Our LEADERSHIP JOURNEY

Shared Stories, Lessons, and Advice for Women of Color

By Dr. Waajida L. Small

OUR LEADERSHIP JOURNEY: SHARED STORIES, LESSONS, AND ADVICE FOR WOMEN OF COLOR. Copyright 2020 by Waajida L. Small. All rights reserved.

No part of this publication may be reproduced, distributed, or transmitted in any form or by any means, including photocopying, recording, or other electronic or mechanical methods, without the prior written permission of the publisher, except in the case of brief quotations embodied in critical reviews and certain other noncommercial uses permitted by copyright law.

For permission requests, write to the publisher, addressed "Attention: Permissions Coordinator," 205 N. Michigan Avenue, Suite #810, Chicago, IL 60601. 13th & Joan books may be purchased for educational, business or sales promotional use. For information, please email the Sales Department at sales@13thandjoan.com.

Printed in the U. S. A.

First Printing, August 2020

Library of Congress Cataloging-in-Publication Data has been applied for.

ISBN: 978-1-953156-0307

DEDICATION

To my mother, Pamela, and grandmother Ella. I am who I am because of your love and encouragement.

And to all of the women on a journey to be better for themselves, their families, their community, and the world...

"Our deepest fear is not that we are inadequate. Our deepest fear is that we are powerful beyond measure. It is our light, not our darkness that most frightens us. We ask ourselves, 'Who am I to be brilliant, gorgeous, talented, fabulous?' Actually, who are you not to be?"

- MARIANNE WILLIAMSON

TABLE OF CONTENTS

INTRODUCTION.. 1

PART ONE

Chapter 1
The RIO Leadership Model 11

Chapter 2
Defining Leadership: What It Is and Isn't-Multiple Perspectives 23

PART TWO

Chapter 3
Understanding People to Better Lead Them 35

Chapter 4
Leadership- From Our Vantage Points 49

Chapter 5
So Many, But Not Enough- Why There Are So Few Women of Color in Leadership Roles 59

PART THREE

Chapter 6
The Reality of Perception 71

Chapter 7
The Fear Within 85

Chapter 8
Being Perfectly Imperfect 95

Chapter 9
The Balancing Act.. 105

PART FOUR

Chapter 10
Making Connections and Creating Safe Spaces 119

Chapter 11
Developing Your Social Capital... 127

Chapter 12
Become Your Sister's Keeper 135

Chapter 13
Channeling Your Elders Mentorship, Sponsorship and your Virtual Board of Directors 143

PART FIVE

Chapter 14
Becoming Who You Were Meant to Be 159

Chapter 15
Finding the HERO Within 167

Chapter 16
Stepping Out and Stepping In - Living Your Purpose 177

Epilogue 187

Acknowledgments 193

30 Day Reflection 197

Appendix A 231

Appendix B 234

Participant Questionnaire Results 238

Endnotes 243

INTRODUCTION

"Your journey has molded you for your greater good, and it was exactly what it needed to be. Don't think you've lost time. There is no short-cutting to life. It took each and every situation you have encountered to bring you to the now. And now is right on time."

— Asha Tyson

Our Leadership Journey: Shared Stories, Lessons, and Advice for Women of Color began as a reshaping of my doctoral research. The goal of my research was to identify the self-limiting factors that prevented women of color from emerging as leaders. As I thought about the many topics that I could explore, I engaged in some deep self-reflection. I asked myself what was important. What do I want to know and learn? What knowledge would I like to share with others? To which field of study do I want to contribute? Where can I make the greatest impact?

I thought about my own journey as a professional. What had the greatest influence on me? How did I get to where I was? Where did I want to go? What was I passionate about?

In the Beginning

Prior to undertaking my studies, I had set out on a personal and professional development excursion if you will. I wasn't quite sure what my next steps were going to be, but I knew I wanted to improve my current situation. I started looking into various groups related to my field of work, and women's groups that focused on women's leadership development. At the time, I was a budding leader, so I thought, why not? I would have an opportunity to network, meet new friends, and learn how to better position myself so that I was able to grow within my role and organization. I would also learn how to stop obstructing my own path, which I felt that I had been doing for a long time.

Being a part of these groups, I realized that my passion was helping women navigate the turbulent waters that can be corporate America. Specifically helping women of color, because as we all know… for us, the struggle is extra real. As a "double minority," we are often at the bottom of the barrel. We are consistently seen as being inferior or incapable, and even when we prove ourselves to be more than competent, not only do we have to fight each other, we have to fight everyone "higher on the list" to get what we've worked so hard for.

On the other hand, there are some of us who were "born to lead," as they say, but we choose to stay in the shadows. For quite a while, I was one of those people. I took a backseat when I knew in my heart that I should be leading the charge. I sat quietly while others raised their hands, and I often had to "follow" individuals, who on occasion were leading me off a cliff. I thought about all of these things as I reflected on what to spend nearly two years of my life doing. In the end, I realized that my passion was me. Me as a professional woman of color who faces many internal and external challenges as she journeys to be her best self and be successful and fulfilled in life and work. Me as the woman who was programmed to fear her intellect, her beauty, her strength, and her courage, because those things threatened others. I was passionate about all the women like me who kept themselves from being who they were called to be.

The Research

There were four factors which provided justification for the need to conduct research on the experiences of women of color as they aspire to and ascend into leadership roles, and the reasons why when presented with opportunities to do so, they choose not to.

The first factor was to close a notable gap in the scholarly research literature that informed society, scholars and practitioners alike of the experiences of women of color who seek to obtain leadership roles or positions.

The second was to diversify the perspective of the presently available leadership research. Much of the research that has been conducted in the United States has been carried out by white men and has used the white male experience as a point of reference.

The third reason was to close a gap in the research regarding the effect of stereotype threat on the work experience, leadership emergence, perception of performance, and leadership ability of people of color. I wanted to provide a more informed understanding of the role perception played in the workplace and the effect it had on determining leader ability and credibility.

Finally, my research provided an opportunity to explore intersectionality and the concept of "double jeopardy" for women of color, and the roles each play in the emergence, development, and implied effectiveness of their ability to lead. Specifically, there was an opportunity to view intersectionality and its perpetuation of the barriers faced by women of color via the "glass ceiling," "bamboo ceiling," "concrete wall," "sticky floor," "labyrinth," and ultimately "glass cliff."

There were four questions that informed my research. One overarching question, the "Central Question," and three main guiding questions, or "sub questions."

The central question was what are the reasons why women of color choose not to self-select into leadership roles?

The sub-questions included:

1. What are the lived experiences of women of color on their journeys to attain leadership roles?

2. What are the internal and external factors that prevent women of color from attaining leadership roles?

3. When presented with opportunities to serve in leadership roles, what are the reasons why women of color choose not to take advantage of them?

Where We Stand Today

It is four years from the start of my doctoral studies and three years post research. We are in the present, and my goal has shifted. This book is more than a reshaping of my research. It is a tool for professional women of color and for those who teach, coach, work with, work for, lead, and are led by those women.

For the women who read this book, you will read stories of women who are just like you. You will also be provided with the best advice I can give you to help you navigate the rocky terrain that is the workforce. This advice comes from my experience as a woman of color in the workforce who has climbed the ladder and faced hardships. It comes from the women whose stories I have seen and heard. It comes from what I have learned as a leadership scholar and practitioner. It comes from the helpful advice that I have been given from women who have journeyed before me.

For those who read this book who have a blossoming leader in their lives, you will learn the same. However, in addition, the insight you gain will help you better support those women. You will also learn a few nuggets that will help you navigate some of the challenges you may be facing as you work toward supporting, coaching, and mentoring them.

What You Can Expect

The goal of this book is multifold. First, I aim to provide you with a foundational understanding of what leadership is, in experience and practice.

Second, I will share with you the stories of women like you and me, who are on paths to become great leaders. These stories I share are from the women who participated in my doctoral research study. To ensure the anonymity of the women in the study and for the purposes of this book, I have used pseudonyms.

Third, I will provide you with practical advice to help you overcome the many obstacles that you not only face from others, but also those you place in front of yourself.

A Model of Leadership

All of the above is achieved by following my RIO Leadership Model. I believe that in order to be successful in leading your own life and work and the lives and work of others, you will have to be able to do the following:

Reflect: Engage in deep self-reflection. Take an inventory of yourself, your situation, your environment, your values, and your beliefs to determine where you are and identify where you would like to be.

Invest: Invest in yourself through continuous learning. As a leader, this will never end. Throughout your voyage, you will come across new people, new opportunities, and new experiences. You should not expect to know how to deal with them as soon as you encounter them, so it is important to prepare yourself by learning new skills, developing your knowledge, and enhancing your abilities.

Optimize. Optimize your knowledge, skills, and abilities by sharing them with others. You will learn that leadership is about engagement and exchange. Don't keep what you know to yourself. Pass it on and pay it forward. This is how you will make the greatest impact.

The Lay of The Land

The book has five parts that follow my model. Parts One through Three fall within the reflect phase. Part One provides a definition of leadership. We look at how leadership is traditionally defined, and then explore what it really is in the theoretical and practical senses.

Part Two discusses who we are as leaders. It looks at who we lead, where we lead, and why we lead--and why there aren't enough of us in leadership positions.

Part Three looks at how we hinder our own progress, oftentimes preventing our own upward movement. We also discuss the realities of perception, fear, and stereotype threat and its crippling effects on career mobility.

Part Four is about investing. I discuss ways in which we can invest in ourselves and in each other to not only survive, but to thrive in every environment we are in.

Finally, in Part Five we talk about how we can optimize who we are. I examine what we need to start doing so that we can become the leaders we were meant to be, the ways in which we can live our purpose, and how we can gain the courage to be our best and most authentic selves.

The journey may seem long, but you are not alone. Let's do this together!

PART ONE
Defining Leadership

"Leadership is hard to define, and good leadership even harder. But if you can get people to follow you to the ends of the earth, you are a great leader."

– INDRA NOOYI

CHAPTER 1

The RIO Leadership Model

In the introduction, I made mention of my RIO Leadership model. In Chapter 2, we will go into a deep definition of what leadership is. It may seem a bit unconventional to discuss my leadership model before we define what leadership is; however, understanding the model will provide context for the remainder of the book. As the model flows, so does the book, and so does the processing of the information within.

About RIO

RIO stands for Reflect, Invest, and Optimize. As I briefly explained in the introduction, these are all activities that I believe every leader should engage in to be effective. When considering the various leadership types and styles, RIO is relevant and can be applied to them all. Why? Because any leader who wants to be successful and make an impact knows she cannot be effective at doing so unless others willingly follow her. This requires introspection, the ability to identify her own needs and the needs of her followers; an investment in filling the gaps when they have been identified; and the capacity to pay it forward, teach, and share her knowledge with others.

Below is a simple visual depiction of the model. Like with life, development for leaders occurs in stages that are sequential yet interconnected. Each stage flows into the next, but leaves space for a return into the previous. This is because as leaders, we will constantly find ourselves returning back to each of the stages.

The RIO Leadership Model (Simple) ™

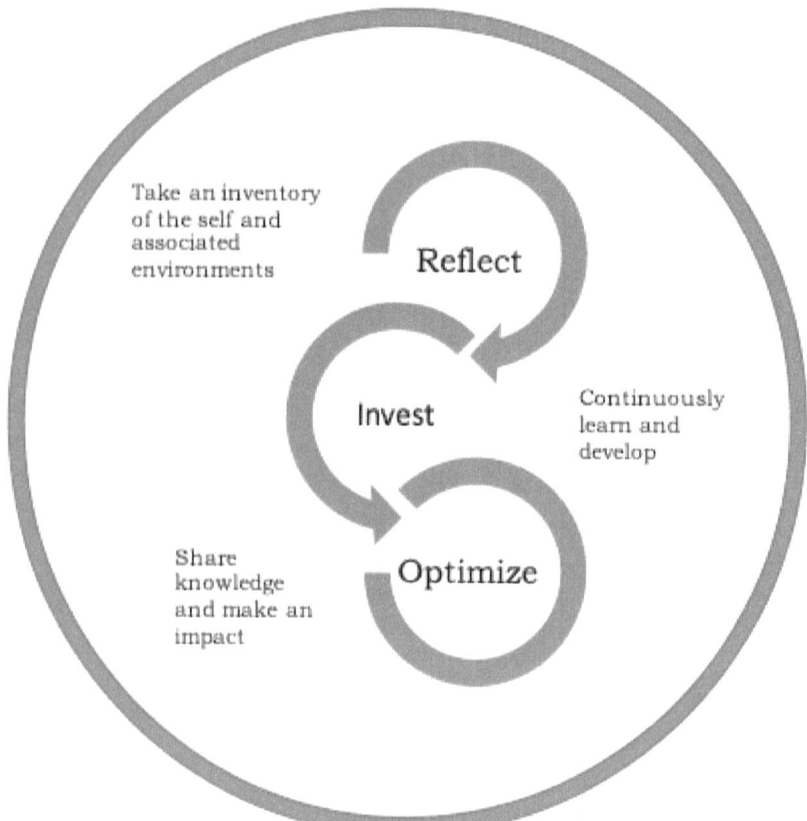

THE MODEL

The first stage in the RIO Leadership Model is Reflect. As leaders, and as individuals in general, being able to engage in self-reflection is a skill that so many lack; and to be quite honest, without it, it is impossible for one to even call themselves a leader. Reflection, by definition, is serious thought or consideration. Reflection, in the context of this model, is the ability to look at one's self and surroundings, assess their current state, and identify the resources needed to reach their desired state. When looking at the self, several factors are taken into consideration. The list is not exhaustive because, as you saw in the visual depiction above, the model is cyclical. As you grow within yourself, as you learn new things, experience new people, situations and environments, and as you engage people and participate in the exchange of knowledge, there will be more to reflect on.

Here is the full RIO Leadership Model™ that shows the interconnectivity of each phase, where they continuously connect allowing for an infinite flow.

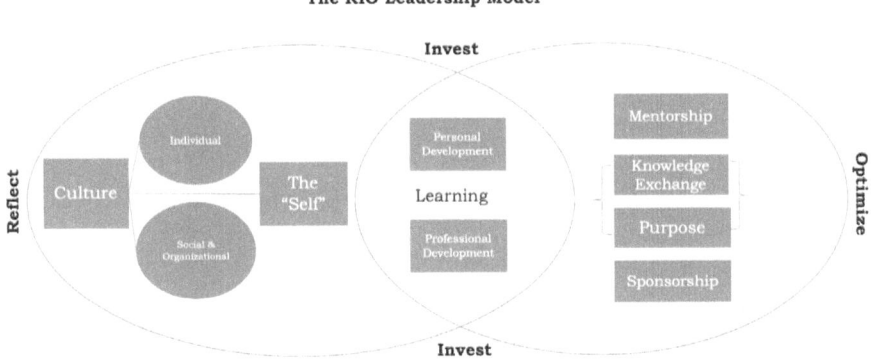

The RIO Leadership Model ™

Reflect

Part of your reflection process as a leader is to question yourself, your values, beliefs, motives, and understanding of people, systems, and processes. This is not questioning yourself in terms of doubting yourself, but more like a self-assessment. As people in general, there are many factors that impact our thoughts, behaviors and actions, and it is important for us to identify what they are before we place ourselves in positions that will impact the lives of others.

Reflect in the RIO Model looks at two key areas:

1. Culture
2. The Self

Culture. Culture in the context of this book is bifurcated and considers primarily individual culture and environment and secondarily societal and organizational culture. Some research suggests that the values and belief systems of individuals impact their effectiveness of the leadership process.[1]

From the perspective of individual culture with culture being defined as: "shared motives, values, beliefs, identities and interpretations or meanings of significant events that result from common experiences of members of a collective that are transmitted across generations,"[2] there are several questions to be asked:

1. What was your upbringing?
2. What are your cultural teachings and beliefs?
3. What values were you taught and now hold?
4. What have been your lived experiences?

Culture regarding society and organizations, while they may seem different, are combined because they are considered external. In much of the research, this is viewed dually: examining societies as individualist vs. collective and masculine vs. feminine. These play a role in whether or not a particular society or organization is viewed as being supportive of the emergence of certain leaders over others.

As we progress in our careers, we are exposed to certain environments, and as we try to navigate through them or move from one to the other, we need to ask ourselves similar questions.

- What have I been taught by this society/organization?
- What are the values of the society in which I live/in organizations that I work?
- What have been my experiences in this society/organization?

There are many questions one must ask themselves as they engage in reflection. Following them all, however, is one central question that is essential to be answered in order to see the growth necessary to be an effective leader: "How have these things impacted my thoughts, behaviors, and actions toward people, systems, and processes?"

The Self. The "self" in the Reflect phase of RIO is inclusive of what I call SCWEEP™. Pronounced "sweep," SCWEEP™ is a reflection on the self in the areas of concept, worth, efficacy, esteem, and perception. How we view ourselves most often, unconsciously, and sometimes consciously, will be projected to and onto others, so it is important as leaders that we have a full understanding of what that is. Ask yourself, what is/are my:

Self-concept—culmination of your thoughts, beliefs, and awareness of who you were, are, and would like to be physically, emotionally, socially, and spiritually.

Self-worth—the value and regard you hold of yourself in spite of what others may say or how they may treat you.

Self-efficacy—belief in your capabilities to perform tasks and influence events (life and/or work) that will produce desired outcomes and achieve the goals you have set for yourself.

Self-esteem—the level of value, approval, and appreciation you have for yourself.

Self-perception—the way you view yourself in relation to others. As with culture, there are several questions to ask in relation to the self, and following each, one final question: "How have these things impacted my thoughts, behaviors, and actions toward people, systems, and processes?"

Invest

The investment phase is at the center of the model with learning as its core. Learning is what facilitates exchange as well as prompts one to engage in reflection of the knowledge they've acquired. In the RIO model, Invest is two-pronged, focusing on personal development and professional development where each impacts the other. Investment in one's own development is critical for growth and, as leaders, the consumption of knowledge is never-ending.

Identifying the need for new learning requires a certain level of awareness that allows an individual to identify where there may be gaps. There should also be an equal amount of desire to fill those gaps. As you would expect, in the second phase of the model, a thorough knowledge and assessment of the self assists in identifying those gaps.

Personal development encompasses an infinite number of areas. Investing in yourself as a person, mentally, physically, emotionally, and spiritually fuels your ability to instill the value of doing so in others. With the goal of any true leader being the ability to inspire others to be their best selves, it is impossible to see that goal realized if they are not following their own advice.

As with personal development, one can develop themselves professionally in various ways. In this book, there is an emphasis on investing in your professional development with regard to creating networks and support systems, and more specifically, increasing your social capital. This is important because it is the value of and investment in the right networks that supports your growth and ensures your relevance as a professional. Additionally, when you consider professional development as it is traditionally viewed, what comes to mind are conferences, networking events, etc. These are places where you meet other professionals in your field for causes that you are passionate about. It is some of those people who will become a part of your network who will invest in you, and you in them.

Investment is defined as the distribution of resources with the expectation of a future benefit. These resources can be tangible, like money or intangible, like emotions. Regardless of the type of investment you have chosen, you must first invest in yourself and your own development before you invest in the development of others. If you initially invest in yourself, you will have built your knowledge and skills strongly enough to where you have a surplus to share with others in need.

Optimize

The final phase of the RIO Leadership Model ™ is Optimize. Optimization means making the best possible use of something.

As leaders, we amass a great deal of resources (knowledge, skills, and abilities) as we move through the phases outlined above. Considering that leadership is an exchange, what better way to make the best use of what we have than to share it with others?

The model identifies four areas within the Optimize phase: Mentorship, Knowledge Exchange, Purpose, and Sponsorship. In future chapters, we will take a closer look at mentorship and sponsorship. For now, we will focus on knowledge exchange and purpose. In short, mentors "turn the lights on" and sponsors make sure they stay on, even when you are not in the room.

You will notice that within the model, knowledge exchange and purpose are centered and connected. This is deliberate, because as a leader, your goal should be to share your knowledge. Being purposeful in doing so is equally important. You will also notice that I've placed them between mentorship and sponsorship. While mentorship can be intentional, most of the time it just happens naturally. It usually starts off when someone sees a set of knowledge, skills, or values that she feels would benefit her, so she approaches the person to teach her. Sponsorship, on the other hand, is usually done intentionally. The person who is the sponsor makes the decision to speak for and act on behalf of the other person.

This may be a lot to take in the onset of the book, but everything will become much clearer in the coming chapters.

LESSONS AND ADVICE

What lessons have we learned?

1. You can't take steps toward getting to know anyone else until you truly know yourself. Engaging in self-reflection is the best mental exercise you can do to prepare yourself to be a leader.

2. Your knowledge, skills, abilities and other attributes are the most valuable assets you have. Investing in the development of each of these will prove to be continuously fruitful.

3. "To whom much is given, much is required"... or something like that. The wisest and most rewarding act you can do is share your knowledge.

My Advice...

Take a step back and do a mental SCWEEP. Reflect on how you view yourself and identify how your own reflection impacts how you view others. We are human and we have egos. When we project certain characteristics or qualities (generally negative) onto others, it is our way of defending ourselves against things we need to improve within ourselves by attributing them to others. We are capable of being biased, and we must be aware of our biases so that we can think and act clearly with the best intentions.

CHAPTER REFLECTION

Take a moment to reflect. Ask yourself...

- What was your upbringing and how has it impacted your thoughts, opinions and actions toward others?

- What are your cultural teachings and beliefs, and how have they impacted your thoughts, opinions and actions toward others?

- What values were you taught and now hold, and how have they impacted your thoughts, opinions and actions toward others?

- What have been your lived experiences as a woman of color?

- What have you been taught to believe about yourself by society or the organization in which you work, and how has it impacted your thoughts, opinions and actions toward others?

- Do a mental SCWEEP. What is/are your levels of:
    - Self-concept?
    - Self-worth?
    - Self-efficacy?
    - Self-esteem?
    - Self-perception?

- What knowledge gaps do you have and what steps can you take to close them?

- What resources do you need to help you get to optimum functionality?

- What knowledge do you have that will be valuable to others?

- How can you be purposeful in your interactions to ensure you are optimizing your knowledge, skills, abilities and other attributes?

CHAPTER 2

Defining Leadership: What It Is and Isn't- Multiple Perspectives

Leadership can be viewed in two ways: firstly, from a technical perspective by way of definition in scholarly research and organizational practice, and secondly by way of demonstration by an individual through their interpretation of what leadership is. However, what is common among both perspectives is the notion of leadership being an exchange. This exchange, in order for it to be effective, has to occur between rational people who are capable of identifying ethical, moral, social, and psychological characteristics in others, and who are willing to follow them to pursue and achieve common goals.[3]

Here's the trouble with that. We are rarely among rational people. Think of the people you interact with on a daily basis at work. Are they all rational? Are they ethically, morally, socially, or psychologically sound enough to assess these characterizations in others? Judging from my own experiences, I would venture to say no. So if the majority of the people you are around at work or in other settings are not capable of identifying the characteristics of what makes a great leader, who are they to judge whether or not you are capable of being one?

They can't.

As women of color, how we are seen, heard, and understood seems to be an anomaly to most. Unfortunately, this may be attributed to the fact that most of the world is seen through the lens of white males. This is inclusive of the concept of leadership. The view of leadership and its perception of associated traits and behavior has created a "prototype" which is seen as white and male, therefore not allowing for anyone who does not fit the prototype to be seen as "leader-like." This view is based on social identity which has its roots in the concept of race.

Race, which many people don't understand, is a social construct. Categorization of people into a "race" was done as a means for exertion of power over "minority" groups, or to ensure equality among other groups. Specifically, the origins of labeling or categorizing groups of people into a "race" category was initiated by Western society who were ignorant and indifferent to the various ethnic and indigenous groups they encountered in Africa and the Americas.[4] According to the American Anthropological Association (AAA) in a 1998 statement on race posted on their website, they argued the following: "'race' as it is understood in the United States of America was a social mechanism invented during the 18th century to refer to those populations brought together in colonial America: the English and other European settlers, the conquered Indian peoples, and those peoples of Africa brought in to provide slave labor." To support their claim that race was a social construct, the AAA provided data which indicated that 94 percent of physical variation lies within racial groups, while there is only a 6 percent difference between racial groups. This shows that there is more of a difference within racial groups than between them.

The social identity approach to leadership states that in order for a leader to emerge, he/she must be seen as being a member of the in-group. Only someone who is a "prototypical" group member will have the highest likelihood of influence and ability to lead the group. If we follow this logic, where being "male" and "white" is the prototype, being female automatically disqualifies a woman as being a part of the in-group, and therefore disqualifies her from being a leader.

Women face many obstacles in their ascension to leadership. These obstacles occur in phases and vary from prevention of emergence to destruction of reign. This is even more so for women of color. These phases have many names, including the "labyrinth," which is the uneven pathway of progression; the "glass ceiling," which is the barrier to getting into "the ultimate" leadership positions; and the "glass cliff," which is being set up for failure once you've reached the top.

Women of Color and Leadership

It is clear that women face several challenges as they seek to emerge as leaders in every context, especially in the organizational context. Women of color, however, face even graver challenges. Research states that women and ethno-cultural minorities confront many leadership challenges. In a hegemonic society like America, those who are not considered to be a part of the in-group, or are seen as "other," are regarded as unlikely leaders.

When leadership is viewed and characterized as being white and male, women of color are considered to be "twice removed" from the leadership power base. This idea of "twice removed" is aptly termed "intersectionality," which is the intersection of gender and race. The challenge with being "twice removed," or identifying with two social "sub categories," is that when you are discriminated against, you don't know if the discrimination is occurring because of one or both of your identities.

Regardless of whether you are female or a person of color, being an "out-group" member on two fronts not only has a negative effect on actual success, but on perceived success as well. Research suggests that when we are part of a diverse workforce (diverse being a relative term), there are constant interactions between different social and cultural groups. In settings such as these, one's own identity, assumptions, and perceptions about others' social or cultural groups have an effect on not only leadership identification, but also on leadership experience. More often than not, the perceptions we have of others and those they have of us are based on stereotypes. Clearly, stereotypes contain attributes that are disadvantageous to leadership.

Common stereotypes of women of color are: the antagonistic and incompetent African-American, the uneducated and unambitious Hispanic, and the quiet and unassertive Asian. For women of color, these stereotypes are elevated to specific "types" of women which are role-based and often perpetuated by popular culture and the media. These stereotypes include "mammy," "sapphire," and "jezebel" when describing African American women, the "geisha girl," "Asian butterfly," or "dragon lady" when describing Asian women, and "hot blooded" when describing Hispanic women.

Being "twice removed" from the dominant group and being stereotyped has proven to cause severe challenges with the leadership emergence of women of color. The greatest challenges include barriers to access and utilization of mentors, having less encouragement to aspire to higher or more visible roles, and not engaging in challenging assignments because of their dual status and separation from the majority culture.

A Picture is Worth a Thousand Words

Leadership Prototype Hierarchy

White Male Heterosexual				Prototype
White Male Homosexual	White Female Heterosexual	Minority Male Heterosexual		Prototype-Subordinate Group
	White Female Homosexual	Minority Male Homosexual	Minority Female Heterosexual	Non-prototypical Subordinate Group
			Minority Female Homosexual	

To understand this visually, let's look at the Leadership Prototype Hierarchy. This hierarchy is based on research which explores the debate of whether or not people who have multiple "subordinate-group" identities experience more discrimination than those with a single "subordinate-group" identity.[5] Social scientists have often argued that race and gender not only affect beliefs about desirability and possibility, but also define the opportunities and life chances an individual has socially and institutionally. Intersectionality or "double jeopardy" has been viewed through several lenses. One of the most popular reviews is the concepts of androcentrism, ethnocentrism, and heterosexism. Androcentrism is defined as "the standard person being male." Ethnocentrism is defined as "the standard person being white," and heterosexism defines the "standard person" as being heterosexual. These identify the "prototype," and those who do not fit these criteria are considered non-prototypical and experience what is called "intersectional invisibility." Intersectional invisibility is the failure to recognize people with multiple social identities (intersecting) as members of the prototypical group. The prototypical group being white, male, heterosexual. So as women of color, since we are not heterosexual white males, we are not recognized.

This prototype hierarchy is reminiscent of what is seen in many organizations. As you can see from the graphic, women of color are "twice-removed" from the "prototype." If you think of the make-up of most organizations (let's say Fortune 500 companies), the top leadership is often a heterosexual white male. Next in the ranks, often in the order depicted above, are more white males (heterosexual and homosexual), white females, and then heterosexual men of color. Middle management is where you will most often see women of color.

After considering the above evidence, you can clearly make the connection between hierarchies within organizations and in society, and the way in which women of color are viewed. We are often seen as incapable and because of this are not provided with access or opportunity. Furthermore, more often than not, we internalize what is projected on us by others, which prevents us from not only seeking out opportunities to lead, but also not taking advantage of opportunities when they are presented to us.

LESSONS AND ADVICE

What lessons have we learned?

1. Those who judge you are generally incapable of making sound judgment, so don't use what others say as a calibration of who you are and what you are capable of doing.

2. Having a better understanding of the underlying context and structures that dictate how organizations and society work allows for better navigation of your environment.

3. Leadership is an exchange. Exchange requires interaction. Interaction can only occur if fear is not present.

My Advice...

Don't allow others to define who you are and who you are meant to be.

Being a leader is about connecting with people on more than just a superficial level. It requires having the ethical, moral, social, and psychological characteristics that others see as strengths and want to gravitate toward. Take advantage of the opportunities presented to you, because it is only through opportunity that you will experience learning and growth! Show the world that there is no "prototype" for leadership, that leadership is not about an individual in a position but the change you can facilitate in others to do better and be better.

CHAPTER REFLECTION

Take a moment to reflect. Ask yourself...

- Are the people you work with/interact with on a daily basis rational? Are they ethically, morally, socially, or psychologically sound enough to assess your character?

- Are you a rational person? Are you ethically, morally, socially, and psychologically sound enough to assess the character of others?

- What are some of the leadership challenges you have faced as a leader or someone on the path to leadership?

- Have you experienced descrimination as someone in a leadership position or on the path to leadership?

- Were you able to determine if the descrimination you faced was because you were a woman or because of your race?

- Have you ever been stereotyped in your role? How has that obstructed your ability to have an impact on others?

- How are you able to connect with people on more than a superficial level?

- Do you take advantage of all of the opportunities presented to you? Why or why not?

PART TWO

Who We Are as Leaders

"There are two powers in the world; one is the sword and the other is the pen. There is a third power stronger than both, that of women."

– MALALA

CHAPTER 3

Understanding People to Better Lead Them

In Chapter 1, we discussed a definition of leadership and how often the lens through which potential for leadership emergence is dependent upon social constructs. While this perspective in most research and practice frequently discusses leadership in the context of organizational leadership, it fails to recognize that leadership and its foundations often occur outside of the workplace.

Who we lead, why we lead, and how we lead as women of color is far more complex than just being a supervisor, manager, or executive in our places of work. The foundation of our desire to lead and guide others on successful paths often has its roots in our cultures. The instinct for collaboration and working together to achieve a collective goal is grounded in the philosophy of who we are as individuals and, historically, where we come from.

Let's think back to the definition of leadership and how the perspective has always been white and male. When we look at the lens through which anything is viewed, we must always see it as flawed because there is never just one way to view anything or anyone. As viewers, we must have a deeper understanding of the situations, people, places, or things we encounter before we can make any solid judgments or try to understand how to adjust.

The Philosophical Aspects of Cultural Difference

In November 1976, Dr. Edwin Nichols presented his manuscript titled "The Philosophical Aspects of Cultural

Differences" at the World Psychiatric Association in Ibadan, Nigeria. Since its introduction, Dr. Nichols' model has been used across the globe in the teaching and understanding of cultural differences. Having a deeper understanding of one's self and others as culturally different is extremely important because it provides a mechanism for identifying, assessing, and changing the behavior of ourselves and others. It allows us to understand the knowledge, attitudes, and behavior of those who we may see as supporters and those who may be detractors.

Dr. Nichols groups multiple ethnicities by identifying four groups he believes share world views. The first group is comprised of European and European Americans. The second includes African, African Americans, and Hispanic/Latinos. The third group consists of Asians, Asian Americans, Polynesians, and Native Americans. The fourth and final group includes Mediterranean and Middle Eastern.[7] For each of these groups, their historical worldviews are broken down into four factors: (1) Axiology (2) Epistemology (3) Logic (4) Process.

I want to provide you with a deep understanding of the differences among cultures, and conversely, the similarities we share. I want to do this first by providing you with a background of the four factors attributed to the worldviews of the cultures as identified by Dr. Nichols. It is important for you to understand these because they provide a basis for the thoughts, behaviors, and actions of individuals, including yourself. Once you are done reading this, and, if needed, have done some of your own research, I want you to self-reflect on your own thoughts, behaviors, and actions and how these factors contribute to them.

Axiology. On a micro level, axiology is the study of values. What do we value as individuals, as a culture, or in relation to home, family, work, etc.? Our axiology as individuals usually comes from our upbringing, is generally historic in nature, and collectively, as "same or similar peoples," creates our culture. It is influenced by how and what we are taught in our homes, communities, houses of worship, and our interpretations of these teachings. Our axiology, or system of values, is one of the greatest influences on how we behave and how we interpret the behaviors of others. Being unfamiliar with the axiology of other people and cultures, we often take the wrong approach when dealing with them. This causes conflict, confusion, and frustration.

From an organizational perspective, understanding the axiology of those you work with, work for, and who work for you is a necessity for optimal performance. This knowledge will inform you of the best way to navigate the workplace. Knowing how to speak, interact with, manage, and network with people from an axiological standpoint will give you the greatest advantage in every situation. You can be strategic with every move. Don't get me wrong; you should always be genuine. Don't be fake, because fakeness always comes to light, and as an individual you will lose credibility. But you must be smart. Reach people at their core levels. If they value straight and to the point, be straight to the point. If they value relationships, build relationships.

This goes for those that approach you as well. They will most likely not have a clue about you, who you are, or what you value. However, with your knowledge of them, you will know how to respond appropriately so that the outcome will be in your favor. When you already know someone, you don't have to stress yourself trying to figure them out. I can guarantee that many of us on too many occasions have said to ourselves or others, "I just don't understand him/her. Why does he/she do, say, act that way?" Now you will know.

As leaders, understanding people at their core is crucial. It helps you reach them on a level they understand and provides opportunity to focus on developing them, not just dealing with them. It is common knowledge that leaders do not exist without followers. No one wants a reluctant follower. Reluctant followers slow progress and, in some cases, intentionally try and stop it. No, leadership is not easy. It's not meant to be. However, detractors among followers can make effective leadership almost impossible.

Epistemology. The simple definition of epistemology is the way of knowing. According to the Stanford Encyclopedia of Philosophy,[8] the following are guiding questions related to epistemology:

- What are the necessary and sufficient conditions of knowledge?
- What are its sources?
- What is its structure, and what are its limits?
- How do we understand the concept of justification?
- What makes justified beliefs justified?
- Is justification internal or external to one's own mind?

Dr. Nichols identified three components of epistemology:

1. applied –the lens through which information is understood
2. pedagogy- the practice used to teach or share information
3. methodology- the methods used to teach/share information

As individuals, understanding the epistemology of those we encounter allows us to "speak their language." How, when, and what we communicate makes all the difference in whether we will be understood. While in any setting everyone may speak the same language, e.g. English, Spanish, French, etc., depending on whether or not you speak words that resonate on a cellular level will determine if your message gets across.

As leaders, this is especially important. When we are in positions of teachers, trainers, and coaches, we must communicate in ways that will be understood so that our words become actionable. Think of it in terms of learning. Adults learn differently than adolescents. The method of teaching has to be appropriate for your audience. If the person with whom you are communicating understands a certain style of language or processes information differently, to ensure he/she learns what you are trying to teach, you have to teach the way in which he/she learns best. This is a skill that needs to be developed. However, once mastered, you will find it much easier to communicate with more ease with those you previously found to have difficulty understanding you.

Logic. The way in which we think about or understand things is logic. It is our mode and principles of reasoning. It is the internal compartmentalization of information to make it easier for us to process and, ultimately, respond to or act on. This is the most straightforward concept; however, it can be the most difficult to understand as an observer of behavior or as someone interacting with other individuals or groups who seem to have "flawed logic." It's just how they understand things.

I can't stress enough the importance of knowing someone else's logic. The truth is, you may never understand the 'WHY' of their logic, but you don't need to. You need to be able to understand the 'HOW.' Knowing how information will be understood and processed will allow you to be proactive in anticipating the response you might receive. You may even be able to predict a response. You will know what was not understood, what type of follow-up will be required, and identify whether or not there may be the potential for conflict due to misunderstanding.

Process. This is the practice of reasoning. Our process informs our interactions. From a philosophical perspective, process is the progressive course of reasoning which results in action. These are the steps we take to achieve a desired end goal. Process is the actionable steps employed based on what we value, how we know our values to be justified, and our reasoning of that justification. Process also includes the "tools" or "instruments" we use to support us in achieving our end goal.

Using yourself as an example, think of your process. Do you have a creative process? Is your process repetitive? Is it mental, physical, or both? Do you follow a routine? Do you know people who have processes like this?

How people go about doing their work is their process. When you understand a person's process, you will better understand why you are getting (or not getting) the results you are seeking. An individual's process will dictate what an eventual outcome will be. Have you ever wondered why you always see the same type of work from someone--perhaps it seems as if it is always the status quo? It is because of their process.

As you will start to understand, axiology, epistemology, logic, and process are sequential. Each one informs its successor, provides insight into who an individual is, and explains why people act the way they do. When you begin to understand individuals and groups on these primal levels, you will start to adjust your approach. Your interactions will become less complicated, you will find yourself less frustrated, and you will be in a better position to lead because you will know your followers.

Ethnic Worldviews

Now let's talk about specifics. As you read about the various world views of different ethnicities, I want you to think about those you encounter at work or in other professional and social settings. As you do this, you will begin to have moments of clarity. Things will start to click. You will begin to remember conversations you've had with a co-worker or recall an interaction at a meeting or event. And as you recall these events, you will also start to strategize about how your approach to a situation or reaction will be different during the next encounter. As a leader of a team, you will start to understand your team members better and begin to identify new methods of teaching and coaching them, as well as formulate plans on how to achieve better group cohesiveness. You will also learn about yourself. You will come to several realizations that will also help you better understand your own thought process and behavior.

I encourage you to take notes as you read through this next section. Write down what you don't understand so that you can do some additional research to learn more. You should also write down where you want to do a deeper dive into what you do understand, even if only for your own edification. You will be surprised at the change you will see when you begin to understand people at their core. As a leader, you will be better equipped to assess people, their values, motives, and ways of thinking and learning so that you can be more effective in leading them.

Europeans and European Americans

Axiology: Member-Object

Value is placed highest on objects or the acquisition of objects. Self-worth is generally determined by the number, size, or monetary value of objects.

Epistemology: Counting and measures

Applied: Knowledge is gained through counting and measuring

Pedagogy: Identifying the parts to the whole

Methodology: Knowledge is shared linearly and sequentially

Here, knowledge is often gained by measuring what can be ascertained by the senses (it only exists if I can see it, smell it, taste it, feel it, etc.) or can be proven by "mathematics" or science. The concept of a "gut feeling" is generally not accepted.

Logic: Binary/ Either-Or

The logical process is that of standardization, codification, precisions, and uniformity.

Process: Everything is repeatable and reproducible

Think of the concepts of producing widgets or an assembly line process. Everything is standard, there is little room for creativity or deviation from what has been established.

Africans, African Americans and Hispanic/Latino

Axiology: Member-Member

Value is most often placed in interpersonal relationships. How one views themselves is determined by the quality of the relationships they have and how others view them. This often perpetuates the idea of needing to be perfect. This idea of perfection or needing to know everything before one can move forward in a role stems from this axiology that women of color find themselves stressing over. The notion of being "every woman" comes from this as well.

Epistemology: Imagery and pattern recognition

Applied: Knowledge is gained through symbolism and rhythm

Pedagogy: Seeing the "Big Picture"

Methodology: Knowledge is shared using a critical path analysis and is communicated in a very "cut to the chase" way

Knowledge acquisition occurs most frequently through feeling and intuitions. Considering the notions of seeing the "big picture" or the whole, appearance is very important. How someone presents their intentions through external behaviors is a telling sign. For example, think of a time when you interacted with someone and your impression of them was that they were not being genuine. What did they say or do that gave you that impression? There is an innate use of the senses.

Logic: Diunital- Both/And

The logical process identifies the union of opposites and "the in-between."

Process: Everything is interrelated through human and spiritual networks. One example is the Black church.

In its simplest explanation, the process and logic for this group runs on the idea of nothing existing without the other. There is no Black without white, there is no good without bad, and there is no heaven without hell. There is an inherent spirituality, as well, and this is incorporated into every aspect of life.

Asians, Asian Americans, Polynesians and Native American

Axiology: Member-Group

Value is placed highest on what benefits the group as a whole. Individual self-worth is associated with connectedness and oneness with the earth and nature. The understanding of others in relation to "something more" is then applied to people and situations.

Epistemology: Transcendence

Applied: Knowledge is gained through transcendental striving. The idea of "seeing the tree through the forest."

Pedagogy: The whole and the parts are seen simultaneously.

Methodology: Knowledge is shared through cycles and repetitions.

Knowledge acquisition occurs through transcendental experience by means of meditation or entering alternative states of consciousness. This allows the individual to connect themselves as a part to the whole in order to gain enlightenment and insight.

Logic: Relative

The world is often conceived independent of thought and mind.

Process: Everything is independently interrelated in the harmony of the universe.

Harmony is probably the most important word in summarizing the above. Inherent within these cultures is the concept of oneness. Being one, whether it is with the family, universe, or environment, is important for self-identification and acknowledgment. Notions such as reincarnation and karma are very important. Because "what goes around comes around" is core in their teachings, you will find that kindness is an almost natural occurring characteristic.

Mediterranean & Middle Eastern

Axiology: Member-Scripture/Spirit

For this group, values are placed highest on scripture or the sacred text of or about a divine being. How an individual views himself/herself is based on the level to which they adhere to the sacred. If he/she lives by the word, they are then worthy of the good they receive, and vice versa.

Epistemology: Code

Applied: Knowledge is gained through reflection and spiritual receptivity.

Pedagogy: The whole is seen through experiential reflection.

Methodology: Knowledge is shared through spiritual teachings that are passed down generations.

Knowledge acquisition occurs through spiritual teachings

that are passed down through generations. Generally, there is no separation of scientific knowledge and spiritual knowledge.

Logic: Prescribed The logical process is determined by what is defined by scripture.

Process: Everything is interrelated and connected to a higher power.

For this group, nothing exists without the "higher power." Whether this power is called God, Allah, or Yahweh, nothing and no one is above him. While they may be "led" by others in the organizational context, it is important to understand that their belief is only by this higher power. If they feel that you are being disingenuous, or your conduct or behavior is contrary to what is prescribed as "righteous," they will be expressive of their disagreement with your behavior. As they live by the rule of the scripture, you will often find that in the workplace, they are very stringent on following established policies and procedures and have difficulty deviating from them.

Why did I go into all of these specifics? The answer is simple. If you do not understand people beyond what you see on the surface, you will be at a disadvantage. The organizations and the communities where we live are not uniform environments; therefore, our thinking and understanding of people cannot be homogeneous either.

LESSONS AND ADVICE

What lessons have we learned?

1. Knowing who people are at their core, what their motives are, how and why they say certain things, and why they behave the way they do is advantageous to you. This knowledge allows you to be more strategic in your approach to people and building relationships.

2. Individual ethnic worldviews define and dictate behavior. If we want to be effective at managing and leading individuals, we have to understand these behaviors so that we know how to manage them as well.

3. We are not all the same; however, there are some of us who share similar values.

My advice...

Get out of the habit of seeing things from only your own point of view. You and your people are not the only ones that exist, and if you have any intention of being a successful leader, you should get to know the needs of your followers. As women, we share the commonality of gender. As women of color, we share the commonality of discrimination. As women from varying cultural backgrounds, we are different, and in order for us to effectively work together to lift each other up and to make effective impacts on the environments we are in, we have to understand those differences so that we can lead them.

CHAPTER REFLECTION

Take a moment to reflect. Ask yourself...

- What do you value as an individual, within your culture, or in relation to your home, family, work, etc.?

- How do you understand and process information?

- What are the necessary and sufficient conditions for you to acquire knowledge?

- What are your primary sources of knowledge?

- What is the structure of your learning, and what are its limits?

- How do you understand the concept of justification?

- What makes justified beliefs justified?

- Is justification internal or external to your own mind?

- Do you have a creative process? Is your process repetitive? Is it mental, physical, or both? Do you follow a routine? Do you know people who have processes like yours?

- Do you believe your ascribed culture to be true and accurately reflective of your beliefs and way of interaction?

- How would you define your axiology, logic and process?

CHAPTER 4

Leadership- From Our Vantage Points

We are fierce leaders! While there are many who may try to deny it, we must not deny it to ourselves. If we are to be honest, leadership comes naturally for women of color. For centuries, we have led our families, tribes, even dynasties, and we've been the most effective at it. We lead in our communities, we lead movements, and we lead organizations. When we look at it from an anthropological perspective, there are many tribes, in Africa, Asia, and the Americas that are matrilineal. There are also many historical and current societies that are matriarchal. Matrilineal meaning from the maternal line and matriarchal meaning women hold primary power.

In his book, "Leadership in a Diverse and Conflicted World,"[9] Dr. John P. Fernandez examines the history of leadership. He writes of early human history and discusses the tight knit and egalitarian way of living. He specifically notes that leaders were chosen based on competence, generosity, fairness, and compassion. He stated that while society has since changed, what we seek to find in a good leader has not. Now, if I recall correctly, those are the exact traits that are often used to characterize women.

In Chapter 1, I mentioned how leadership can be viewed two ways; the first being from a technical perspective by way of definition supplied by scholarly research and organizational practice. Second, by way of demonstration by an individual through their interpretation of what leadership is. As women of color, we have a very unique perspective of leadership. This is because leadership is not just about a group of people we are responsible for at work. It is about what we value, the relationships we develop and cultivate, the impact we have on others, and the growth we foster in ourselves and those around us.

How We See Leadership

Leadership for women of color is more than just being in the office or the boardroom. Who we lead, why we lead, how we lead, and how we define leadership is rooted in our culture, our upbringing, and our experiences.

During my doctoral research, I had the opportunity to interview several women. The interviews focused on their experiences as women of color who were either aspiring to, on their journey to, or having reached leadership status as defined by scholars and current organizational and societal practices. These women varied in age, education level, and profession, which provided very unique perspectives.

One central question that was asked of all of the women was, "How do you define leadership?" As a follow-up question, I asked them, based on their definition of leadership, if they considered themselves to be leaders. I asked these questions for several reasons. The first was to identify whether or not there were variances in the definition based on their professional level. The second was to identify if there were variances in the definition based on their cultural and ethnic make-up (because culture influences belief and behavior). The third reason was to identify if their definition was similar to how society defines leadership (because society influences behavior). The final reason was to determine what questions I would ask next that would allow me to dive deeper into their stories.

Throughout the coming chapters, I will share the stories of several women and their experiences as women of color who are on a leadership journey. I am starting with the stories of Mariah H. and Wilma M. While all of the women who participated in interviews provided very profound definitions of leadership, I thought these two were very reflective of the interplay of life, culture, and experience. They will also be able to provide some context to all of the stories I will share.

As you read these stories and how these women defined leadership, ask yourself the same questions. How do you define leadership? And, based on your definition, do you consider yourself a leader?

Reflecting on how you define leadership will help prepare you to become a better leader. It will help you identify your beliefs and values and determine whether or not you've been effective thus far.

MARIAH H'S STORY

Mariah is 35 years old. She is what you would consider a social entrepreneur. She has held several leadership roles in both for-profit and non-profit organizations. She is a first-generation Latina who, as she describes, did not come from an affluent family and whose journey was not easy. During our interview, Mariah was very open and honest about her upbringing and the challenges she faced, as well as how those challenges have shaped who she is today.

> "As a Latina, I don't come from an affluent family. I don't have the networks that others are privileged to have. I don't - I had to learn that myself. Being out there, networking, talking to people, putting in the work - it's kind of like that self-promotion aspect that is, I'd say it's a little shunned in our culture because we're very, at least my upbringing was, that we have to be very modest. We have to be very humble. We cannot be very ostentatious."

Mariah was brought up to be modest, humble, and told never to be ostentatious. For her, self-promotion was frowned upon, and early on this had a negative impact on her growth. She was often told that a young lady should never make herself the center of attention. But as Mariah embarked on her journey to become a sought-after expert in international and global affairs, focusing on human rights, she learned the value of connecting with people and building relationships. These connections have put her at the helms of boards, committees, and now her own multimedia and social impact consultancy that helps clients in the public, private, and social sectors.

When asked, "How do you define leadership, and based on your definition, do you consider yourself to be a leader?" Here is how Mariah responded:

> "*[**Leadership is**] the ability to get things done in a way that moves people, drives them to excel, and [allows them] to demonstrate their own personal excellence. Leadership, to me, is being able to inspire excellence in others. I think leadership is very unique to every individual. I think every person has that ability to be a leader and to develop leadership.*
>
> *"[I consider myself to be a leader because] I get things done. I'm able to mobilize people from diverse sectors. Most importantly, [I can influence] people who don't even agree with me to come to the table and get things done. I would consider myself very inclusive. I warmly welcome people to engage with me, and to disagree with me. I think that's the most important thing. I don't have all the answers, and [it's] okay not to have answers. [As a leader] I want people to challenge me. I want people to bring their best ideas and their most authentic selves forward, and bring it to the table, so we can get the best product, or the best final idea out there. I do think that as a leader, you need to be very introspective. You need to reflect on why you're making the decisions and be okay with being yourself. I love getting to know people. I like understanding where they are coming from, their work styles."*

Mariah sees leadership as influence, impact, and collaboration. Authenticity is central to who she is and she encourages it in those she works with and those she leads. Her approach to leadership is very much aligned with her axiology. Building relationships and being collaborative is how she leads best. Her ability to build relationships also allows her to impact those who may disagree with her approach, but it is her collaborative nature that influences them.

WILMA M'S STORY

Wilma is an African American woman in her early 60s. She's had a successful career in the media, marketing, and sales sectors for many years. After graduating with her bachelor's degree from a university in the Midwest, Wilma set out for NY. Once in NY, she landed several positions where she managed accounts in multiple forms of media, fashion, and marketing. As an older African American woman in the workforce, Wilma has and still faces many challenges. Discrimination for her occurs on three fronts: first, being African American; second, being a woman; and third, being an older worker.[10] Discrimination has been something WM has had to deal with most of her life, especially as she grew up during the Jim Crow Era. However, as an African American woman, coming from a culture where women often take on the dominant role in the family, Wilma has persevered in tremendous ways.

For Wilma, the generation in which she was born has also played a role in her development as a leader. For women of the Boomer generation, expectations were very different. To be frank, the expectation for an African American woman of that generation did not include leadership anywhere outside of the home.

> *"I think that when you come from [our] culture, in many instances you may be educated, but you realize that there are a lot of obstacles in your way. A lot of times there are just so many, [and] sometimes it gets a little bit overwhelming. I think a lot of women, at some*

point [think] maybe they should start a family or they start thinking that here are some things in my life that are more important to me- do I really want to go this corporate route and maybe not have a family, or do some of the things that I want to do in my lifetime? Which ones are more important? I think, a lot of times, in many instances, women of color choose [to forgo career success]."

Wilma, while struggling with the decision of career or family, managed to find a way to have both. She was not deterred by the expectations placed on her because of her gender, ethnicity, or the generation in which she was born.

When asked, "How do you define leadership, and based on your definition, do you consider yourself to be a leader?" Here is how Wilma responded:

"[From my perspective], leadership has changed quite a bit over the years. At this particular point in time I think it has a lot to do with the organization that you're working with. I think that it's changed from the position of more of a dictatorship type situation where things are pretty much set to a more open conversation and understanding about which way the organization might need to go, the direction it needs to go in, and how it needs to be ongoing as far as success goes. I think it's a little bit more of an interaction between a team and a leader.

[Regarding would I consider myself a leader] That's an interesting question, because I've asked myself this, especially recently. I think I'm a team player. I think that at certain times, any kind of initiation, be it business, if you're doing initiatives to build revenue or whatever, I think it's important to allow each person

who has the best critiques to be the leader. I think when you're a little bit open to allowing that to shift itself a bit, you are able to work better as a team. I know in most situations, you do have someone that is an executive head or someone who is leading a team, but situations that I think are [the most] successful [are situations where people] are allowed to share information, research, and permit [others] to emerge as leaders that may not always be the leader of that particular team."

Wilma's definition of leadership shows similarities to that of Mariah. From an axiological perspective, Wilma describes the interaction between leader and followers (leader and team) which is illustrative of the importance of relationships. Her definition and description of how she sees herself as a leader is also reflective of her logic in the emphasis on the distinction between leader and team.

Mariah and Wilma are only two women of many who have provided their definition of leadership. Because they share similar cultural worldviews, there are similarities in their definitions. However, taking into consideration the differences in their upbringing, career stages, and ages, the perspectives they have on leadership and what it looks like is different. Their own views of themselves as leaders are also different. Why does that matter? It matters because even amongst ourselves there are differences, and if we want to work together to change the similar challenges we face, we need to be able to work together. The only way to work together effectively is to understand what our differences are.

LESSONS AND ADVICE

What lessons have we learned?

1. We are a force to be reckoned with. It is in our DNA to lead. We need to channel our ancestors for guidance and courage when we begin to doubt our ability.

2. It is okay to have your own definition of leadership. How you define leadership is based on your experience and worldview. Both of those things will be different for everyone; therefore, everyone's definition of leadership will be different.

3. It is all about perspective. Just because you may see something differently than someone else or have had different experiences doesn't mean that you don't share common values.

My advice...

Embrace your uniqueness. Do not conform to the status quo. Approach every situation with a fresh pair of eyes, but do not change who you are. The individuality you bring to a team, group, or organization is what makes you qualified to be in the position that you are in. Always take into consideration the individuality of others, especially those you lead. Whether you are appointed as a leader or you are sought out as one, stay true to you and never compromise your values.

CHAPTER REFLECTION

Take a moment to reflect. Ask yourself...

- How do you define leadership?

- Do you consider yourself a leader based on your definition?

- What are the characteristics of a great leader?

- What characteristics do you have that you believe make you an impactful leader?

- What do you value as a leader?

- How do you cultivate relationships?

- How do you measure the impact you have on others?

- How do you foster growth in yourself and others?

CHAPTER 5

So Many, But Not Enough- Why There Are So Few Women of Color in Leadership Roles

There is no denying that we are magical! As women, especially women of color, we can do just about anything, including rule nations as queens, prime ministers, and chancellors. According to a 2014 Catalyst, women of color were 35 percent of the total population of women in the United States. This is expected to increase to 48 percent by the end of 2020. The number of women of color expected to enter into the workforce from 2014-2024 is expected to significantly increase, with the expectation for Hispanic women to be 30 percent, African American women 24 percent, and Asian women 11 percent.[11] According to a study by the Center of American Progress, there will be a net growth of 117 percent[12] of people of color entering into the workforce, with the majority of them being women of color.

As the saying goes, "We out here!" If that's the case, why are we so underrepresented in leadership roles across the spectrum? According to the same Catalyst report noted in the previous paragraph, women of color make up only 19.8 percent of all board seats held by women in Fortune 500 companies and only 4.5 percent of executives and senior level officials. There is literally only one Latina CEO and one female Asian CEO. We lost the first African American female CEO of a Fortune 500 company in 2016, when pioneer Ursula Burns stepped down from her role at XEROX.

So what is going on, ladies?

In the introduction, I mentioned that my research focused on one central question with three subquestions.

Central Question: What are reasons women of color choose not to self-select into leadership roles?

Subquestions:

1. What are the lived experiences of women of color in their journeys to attain leadership roles?

2. What are the internal and external factors that prevent women of color from attaining leadership roles/positions?

3. When presented with opportunities to serve in leadership roles, what are the reasons why women of color do not take advantage of them?

While the research primarily focused on the self-limitations (which we will discuss in Part Three of the book), the subquestions tried to identify both the internal and external factors that prevent our emergence into leadership positions. From a review of the scholarly literature and listening to the experiences of the women who participated in the study, the environments that we are in play a major role in whether or not we will be able to realize our full potential and emerge as leaders.

When we take into account environmental factors, there are what are considered emergence supporters and emergence deterrents. Emergence supporters are those that allow us to flourish, emerge as leaders, and take advantage of leadership opportunities. Emergence deterrents are just the opposite. These are the factors that hinder our advancements. The diagram on page 61 illustrates a section of the model I have created that identifies the emergence supporters and emergence deterrents in relation to women of color.

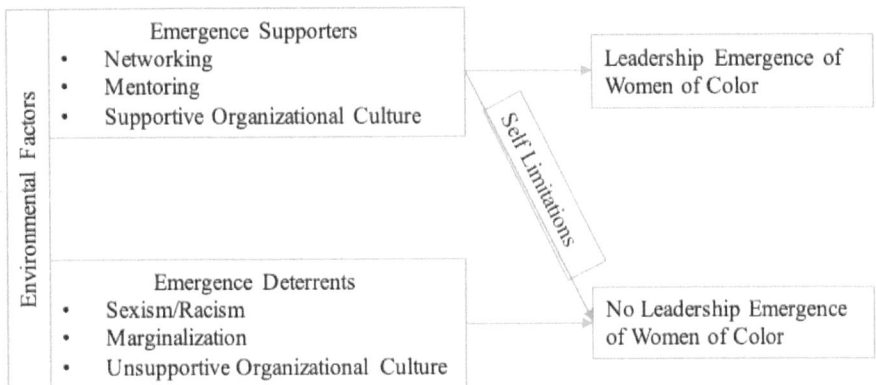

Some of the environmental factors that support our emergence as leaders are networking, mentoring, and a supportive organizational culture. Deterrents include sexism and racism, marginalization, and an unsupportive organizational culture. One would expect that this is all obvious; however, to be quite honest, it is not. Most of us only focus on the things that stand out the most, e.g. both overt and covert racism, sexism, and marginalization. We rarely ever take a hard look at whether or not the overall environment and culture of an organization is supportive of our development.

How is our Environment Relevant to our Emergence as Leaders?

Most of the leadership research, in particular those that focus on trait-based leadership, has in some ways failed to consider the relationship between the environment and leadership emergence. Much of the literature discusses the organizational environment as being a supportive and facilitating factor in the development of leaders, and it should be seen as equally as important as the traits a potential leader has. Research continues to suggest that by having a supportive, empowering, and enabling environment, organizations will have better results in intra-organizational emergence and greater long-term leadership effectiveness. Supportive environments are defined as being characterized by a culture and values that encourage leadership emergence.[13]

Further, research identifies five behaviors that organizations can engage in to create an environment that supports leadership emergence.

1. Showing support through the consideration, acceptance, and concern for the needs and feelings of their people
2. Developing emerging leaders through coaching and providing opportunities for skill development
3. Recognizing value through giving praise and showing appreciation for effective performance, achievement, and contributions to the organization
4. Consulting with and involving potential leaders in important decision making
5. Empowering prospects through delegation and providing autonomy and discretion[14]

Supportive organizational cultures are just as important as supportive environments. A supportive culture is one that invests in and enhances the human and social capital of its emerging leaders. This development is fostered by feedback, coaching, mentoring, networks, providing challenging job assignments, and action learning.

You will come across the term mentoring and networking quite a bit in this book, just as I did in my research. Why? Because mentoring and networking have been identified as two of the most successful predictors in leadership emergence.[15] They also have been linked to overall career advancement and success.

We need to be aware of our environments and take a hard look to determine if they are the best places for us. I can definitely say that if a supportive environment is identified by the five behaviors mentioned above, I have yet to be in one. I am quite certain that this is also the case for many of you. The unfortunate truth is that the environments we are in do not support our emergence. Given that this will almost always be the case, we need to find ways to create supportive environments for each other. As the motto of my favorite group, the Black Women of Influence, goes, we need to find ways to "help each other win!" We will discuss some ways we can do this in Part Five.

LESSONS AND ADVICE

What lessons have we learned?

1. We have the skills, and no one can deny it! We are "rolling" deep! There is power in numbers, both literally and figuratively.

2. We are taking over the workforce, and we can use it to our advantage. It is only a matter of time until we will define what the culture of an organization looks like.

3. More than just having the traits of a leader, we must be in a space where we are encouraged to lead.

My advice...

Take stock of your environment. Do a deep assessment of your organization and its culture to determine if it is supportive of your growth. Where you find that there are deterrents, seek out those who can be supportive. If they don't exist, as the saying goes... "Get the hell out of Dodge!" I say that a bit tongue-in-cheek, but you have to consider putting yourself in environments where you will be valued, supported, and cultivated as a leader. I am not saying that organizational culture or environments cannot be changed, but where you find that your environment has a "resistance is futile" mentality, you have to explore other options.

CHAPTER REFLECTION

Take a moment to reflect. Ask yourself...

- What have been your experiences in the workplace?

- What are your environmental supporters and detractors?

- What limitations have been placed on you by the work environment that have prevented your emergence as a leader?

- What limitations have you placed on yourself that have prevented your emergence as a leader?

- What are some of the most recent opportunities for professional growth that have been presented to you? Have you taken advantage of them?

- Why have or haven't you taken advantage of the most recent professional growth opportunities presented to you?

- If you are currently in an organization that does not support your professional advancement, would you consider leaving? Why or why not?

PART THREE

In Our Own Way

"Think like a queen. A queen is not afraid to fail. Failure is another stepping stone to greatness."

– Oprah Winfrey

CHAPTER 6

The Reality of Perception

As I've mentioned previously, there were several themes that emerged from my research. In the preceding chapter, we talked about the external factors that prevent our emergence as leaders. In particular, we discussed unsupportive organizational environments and cultures playing a major role as deterrents in our forward and upward movement in the workplace. In this chapter and the coming chapters of Part Three, we will identify some of the ways in which we play a role in preventing our own growth.

When interviewing the women for the study, there were several themes that emerged as internal, or self-limiting, factors that prevent our emergence as leaders. One of these was the idea of perception. Perception was the most saturated theme, meaning it came up most frequently. Within the theme of perceptions, sub-themes of perception of self, stereotypes, and perception of others appeared.

Research in this area has shown that barriers, including an individual's negative perceptions, motivations, and feelings of self and their abilities are major roadblocks to success. When a woman has a negative perception of herself, those negative views can manifest into actions, which can influence how she is perceived by others.

Stereotypes

The theme of stereotypes revealed itself in two ways throughout the course of the study. The first was in relation to perceived stereotypes, the second, a consciousness of not falling into stereotypes, or as it is commonly termed, "stereotype threat." Often, both consciously and subconsciously, women of color will become the stereotype they work hard trying not to become. This occurs because there is a biased expectation from others. When women of color become aware of these expectations, it is often a challenge not to allow themselves to fall prey to them. They begin to ask themselves, "Should I give them what they expect? If they don't expect more from me, should I give them more?"

There is a quote by Albert Einstein that says,

> "A human being is a part of the whole called by us 'universe,' a part limited in time and space. He experiences himself, his thoughts and feelings as something separated from the rest, a kind of optical delusion of his consciousness. This delusion is a kind of prison for us, restricting us to our personal desires and to affection for a few persons nearest to us. Our task must be to free ourselves from this prison by widening our circle of compassion to embrace all living creatures and the whole of nature in its beauty."

My interpretation is that if people continue to view the world from only their experiences and not take into consideration the experiences of others, the beauty of the world will be lost on them. Beauty, from my perspective, is all-encompassing and includes the value of the knowledge, skills, and abilities one brings to the proverbial "table."

As women of color, especially in the workforce, we are often subjected to stereotypes. We are frequently viewed from a singular lens that is either contrived by people who know nothing about us or perpetuated by people who are afraid that we may take the spotlight. These stereotypes add to our challenges in moving forward and upward.

What is worse, however, is stereotype threat! This is different from actual stereotypes and can be one of the greatest impediments to our success. It is our susceptibility to stereotype threat that is one of the ways we can hinder our own professional growth.

LIZZIE E'S STORY

Lizzie is a proud Latina, a mix of Cuban and Puerto Rican, to be exact. She is "smart as a whip," as the saying goes. One might say that Lizzie, in her young career, has had some great and fast movement as well. Lizzie works for a global women's rights organization where she leads the human resources function. Prior to her role there, she worked for a world-renowned global nonprofit organization for eight years. In those eight years she was promoted three times ultimately ending up in a role as the lead for the HR information systems function. She is the definition of a millennial on the move.

Lizzie was raised by her father and grandmother in a household where women were bosses, but men were kings. Lizzie has two siblings from her mother, but was the only child from her father. As an only child to her father, Lizzie was his queen; however, being raised by a traditional Puerto Rican grandmother who grew up in a culture where "machismo" ruled, being a strong-willed, determined young woman was often frowned upon. Shortly after she completed her undergraduate studies, Lizzie's father passed away. As someone who had often felt out of place in her family because she didn't subscribe to the "norm," Lizzie was left feeling very isolated. In telling me of her journey into her current professional space, she said the following:

> "In my family there's not a lot of professionals. Out of me and my two siblings, I'm the only one who pursued higher education. Out of about 20 first cousins, I am also the only person to pursue higher education, so there were not a lot of examples for me to emulate. I am kind of the first example to do it, so there's not a lot of support from family. I have one friend that I've had since high school who is doing what I'm doing.

The rest, not so much. The community, the family part of it ... I didn't have."

Lizzie has faced many barriers when it comes to a familial support system as she's embarked on her leadership journey. It was also evident that she's faced barriers regarding professional support as well. I asked her what she felt were barriers that women experience in their ascent to leadership, and why.

What I found to be interesting was her mention of stereotypes. While I wasn't surprised she mentioned it, I was surprised that it is so prevalent that it is always at the forefront of our minds when we think of things that can stop our forward movement. As a Latina, she's experienced stereotypes in the workplace firsthand. It is often because of experiences like hers that we become very cognizant of stereotypes, and in our frustration of becoming these stereotypes, we tend to fall prey to them. Lizzie explained it like this:

> *"There are definitely barriers to women, in general, moving up the ladder, if you will. I would have to say, for women of color, there are additional stereotypes that get in your way. In my experience ... If you're a white woman, it's totally different from being a Latina woman or an African American woman because we have additional stereotypes. It's been my experience ... for example, when I was promoted someone asked me if I was educated, and why was I leaving my previous position? Did it require a degree? I was almost sure that the question came from that person in particular because I was a Latina woman versus a non-minority person. I think it came from his assumptions about how he feels about minorities.*
>
> *It's very difficult to be a Latina woman because we have these stereotypes that you know ... if I'm getting promoted, there is this question of is it based on*

my aptitude or skill? Or did I get this role based on flirting with my boss? It's never automatic that it was because of hard work, aptitude, or education.

Also, if I'm strong or opinionated in any given situation, I'm the stereotypical hot-blooded Latina person who cannot control her emotions. Even if I'm expressing an opinion in a rather calm sentiment, or if it's just a digressing opinion from what someone else is expressing. Automatically, it's the crazy Latina, of course, so they don't have to take her opinion seriously. It's one thing to be a woman in an all boys club, but when you add the fact that you're a minority somewhere, there are obviously additional barriers to your growth."

STEREOTYPE THREAT

So what is stereotype threat?

Stereotype threat is having the awareness that there is a lower expectation of your ability to perform based on a perceived image of you rather than your actual performance and, as a result, you begin to fulfill those expectations by presenting weaker performance.[16] Stereotype threat generally occurs when a person cares about something, e.g. becoming a leader, they know that a stereotype exists about the group he/she is a member of, e.g. Latina women, and the stereotype becomes noticeable in a situation where they are required to perform.

Stereotype threat is more likely to occur in the context of three occasions:

1. Difficult or challenging tasks
2. When a stereotype relates to performance
3. When individuals are highly identified with the tasks that are often demonstrated in relation to race/ethnicity,

gender, and social class[17]

Early research noted that individuals are vulnerable to stereotype threat when they know that they run the risk of being viewed in a certain way in a given situation. If we are real with ourselves, as women of color, we are constantly aware of the stereotypes associated with us.

As an African American woman, I have always been conscious of falling into the "angry Black woman" stereotype. Being a human resources professional I constantly find myself having to deal with difficult and challenging people, so it is very easy to fall prey to this stereotype. I have to be stern and limit my emotions so as to not seem partial. And, of course in this role, especially as a Black woman, people will test you, and sometimes intentionally try to bait you.

Stereotypes have severe negative effects on women of color. They cause biases in performance expectations, perceptions of suitability for promotion, and negatively impact the likelihood of receiving training and development for advancement. Not only that, but they also place limitations on access to mentoring and consideration for high-visibility assignments. Stereotypes can also limit or even prevent access to professional growth opportunities like social and professional networks, information, and even support from peers and subordinates.[18] The latter is the most difficult. If even those we are trying to lead see us as stereotypes, how will we get the respect we deserve?

Stereotypes and Stereotype Threat and Leadership

What is the impact of stereotype threat on us as leaders? Many researchers argue that traits reflect the mechanisms by which leaders are selected, and that demonstration of leader behavior is constrained by the situations leaders face. Contradictory to this, however, is the fact that leaders are often identified by others who have limited knowledge of their actual performance. Instead, the identification is based on a perception. When stereotypes are prevalent, though women of color may be qualified for a leadership position, they are often seen as being unqualified and are given limited access to leadership roles.[19] The sad truth is, as women of color in the workplace, we are often viewed as being less capable of being successful and less qualified for leadership positions. Confidence in our abilities to be effective in leadership roles is frequently questioned.

It has been shown that groups who do not normally have access to leadership positions frequently encounter a shift in their beliefs about whether or not they can be effective leaders. Researchers believe this may be due to evidence that leaders of these groups are often evaluated negatively regardless of their performance, which is often the result of stereotyping. Women of color are especially vulnerable before they even begin their journey toward organizational leadership. Stereotype threat can persuade women to avoid leadership roles and settle for "non threatening" subordinate roles.[20]

Unfortunately, the above notion is supported by several Catalyst reports which revealed that racially/ethnically different women were more likely to downsize their aspirations as a consequence of exclusion. The report further found that women of color received fewer promotions, were least likely to be mentored by C-suite and senior executives, and lacked access to career-advancing projects.

Here is Fiona D's story. Hers is one that is not unfamiliar to many of us, but one we can learn from.

FIONA D'S STORY

Fiona is an African American woman in her late 30s. She holds a doctorate degree in public health and has held several research positions at laudable universities. Her roles have included project manager, lead researcher, and co-director, where she was responsible for leading multi-million-dollar research studies. In each of these positions, she has led both projects and teams. Fiona describes herself as a "reluctant leader" who will usually step up if she sees that no one else wants to take the lead.

Fiona has also been in situations where she was stereotyped. In these situations, not only was her leadership style questioned, her ability to lead was put into question as well. This contributed to her current reluctance to be more active in taking on a leadership role. During our interview, Fiona specifically talked about experiencing the "mammie" stereotype. It is often attributed to African American women, and is one of the most commonly known stereotypes. The "mammie" is a mythic female character that is often portrayed as the "always loyal servant to her master's family," and is associated with a slave woman taking care of white children.[21]

During our interview, Fiona spoke about an experience she had as a project manager at a prestigious university. In her role, she was expected to "take care of" the project and ensure that the researchers had what they needed to conduct the research. However, there was the perception that she was also supposed to "take care of" the researchers beyond what was needed to complete the study, like get coffee, etc. Fiona stated:

> "... you're perceived in a certain way, maybe, and I don't have a good word for it other than mammie, right? This whole ... You're there to be somewhat of a caretaker. I'm a project manager, so on some level I'm supposed to take care of a project, but I don't have responsibility to take care of every single person on the team's individual needs."

This perception in some ways made Fiona question her role and whether or not she was supposed to be a caretaker for those working on the research project. When you begin to lose focus on what your role is, you start to underperform, and this may lead to other perceptions. In Fiona's case, she began to feel like the stereotypical mammie. As was revealed later in the interview, Fiona began to question her own ability to do her job, because what she was "expected" to do became muddied.

Further experiences included that of the "angry Black woman," another stereotype primarily attributed to African American women. The "angry Black woman" is the personification of some of what can be considered the worst negative stereotype of Black women including: being out of control, disagreeable, overly aggressive, physically threatening, loud (even when she speaks softly), and to be feared.[22]

Fiona spoke of a specific example where she felt how she was perceived impacted her communication with leadership within her function.

> *"Factors that really impacted my leadership ... Some of it was how I was perceived. I definitely had situations, it wasn't everyone I worked with, but maybe one or two senior people who ... If I would bring up an issue or concern, I would be met with hostility. Some of the same issues would be brought up by potentially my white female coworkers, and it wasn't received the same way."*

For Fiona, based on her observation of her white colleagues addressing similar issues that she had and being received differently, she felt as if she was being viewed a certain way because she was Black. On the other hand, she mentioned later in the interview that her supervisor counseled her on how to soften her language. This instance impacted how Fiona communicated as well. She mentioned becoming self-conscious about how she communicated overall, communication with her own supervisors, and communication with her team.

Perceptions and Actions

How people think of us, and our beliefs of what people think of us, almost always have an impact on how we think of ourselves. Internalizing someone else's perception of us, whether their perception is true or not, can also impact how we behave. Specifically, it can have an impact on the actions we take in advocating for ourselves and our upward mobility. There is always the difficulty in trying to decipher whether or not someone actually has a particular perception of you or if it is your own imagination.

We must constantly be watchful of others' false perceptions

of us and be vigilant not to allow those perceptions to become our reality. Fiona's story is not unique in the sense that there are many young women who have and are experiencing these challenges in the workplace. What's concerning is that, even still, within the millennial generation, women of color are facing an uphill battle. A brilliant young woman who has only ever shown that she is capable has to be fearful of falling into a trap like stereotype threat. She has to waste her time worrying about regressing into a false narrative created by other people instead of focusing on developing herself.

In Fiona's case, having those stereotypes placed on her made her not only question her abilities, but also changed her behavior so as to not be seen as a stereotype. Those experiences greatly impacted how she interacted with colleagues and leaders as she moved along in her career. Fiona felt as if she could not communicate the way she needed to out of fear of how she would be perceived. This prevented her from having the necessary conversations for further career development.

LESSONS AND ADVICE

What lessons have we learned?

1. No one knows us better than ourselves. If we continue to define our own narrative, we won't be susceptible to others' false narratives.

2. Stereotypes are real threats, and stereotype threat is real. We can become what we thought we never would be simply because we are afraid of becoming it.

3. People may project their insecurities on you so that they can feel better about themselves. If you allow their insecurities to become your own, you will lose yourself.

My advice...

Create your own story. Know who you are and embrace yourself. Some people are always going to have something to say about you and what they think you can and cannot do. Those are usually the people who are not qualified to assess your knowledge, skills, or abilities. If you can do a good job of assessing yourself, you will be better able to know who is capable of doing the same. When you realize they cannot, move forward accordingly. Don't fall into the traps of others, and don't create traps for yourself. It is so much easier to give in and give up than fight. We've had to fight all our lives. The sad truth is, we will have to continue to fight for opportunity. The best thing you can do is be properly armed. Be armed with the knowledge of your vulnerabilities and others' insecurities because they can determine what a winning strategy can be. Don't let anyone steal your shine!

CHAPTER REFLECTION

Take a moment to reflect. Ask yourself...

- What stereotypes, if any, have you experienced in your workplace?

- Has experiencing these stereotypes affected your ability to do your work? If yes, how so?

- Has experiencing stereotypes impacted your view on your own ability to do your job effectively?

- Has stereotyping in your workplace prevented you from moving into a leadership role?

- Have you ever believed that you were behaving in a manner that made a stereotype about you true?

- Has your awareness of how people perceive you impacted your behavior?

- Do you believe that a false perception of you has prevented you from opportunities to serve in a leadership role?

- What methods or steps can you take to prevent yourself from succumbing to stereotype threat?

CHAPTER 7

The Fear Within

According to the Merriam-Webster dictionary, the standard definition of fear is "an unpleasant emotion caused by the belief that someone or something is dangerous, likely to cause pain, or a threat." A more technical definition is an emotion caused by specific threat-related stimuli that, in turn, causes a person to adapt their behavior to either avoid or cope with that threat.[23]

From these two definitions, we can confidently say that fear is a discomforting or disagreeable state of mind caused by an actual or perceived threat of harm by someone or something, and, due to that actual or perceived threat, we change what can be considered our "normal" behavior to avoid that threat or deal with it.

Let's put this into context:

Scenario: A young woman is up for a promotion. This promotion puts her in a much more visible position within her organization. She will also be responsible for the performance of others. This is not her first time as a supervisor; however, now her team will be much larger. This position is reporting directly to the chief operating officer, who has been an informal mentor to her for the past three of the five years she has been employed with the company. This role will get her one step closer to becoming senior vice president and leading a global team in a field she is very interested in. She will also have opportunities to network with senior leaders and their connections, which will help her expand her own network.

In this scenario, and in many like it, we as women of color will either hesitate to accept or even decline opportunities like this. One might ask the question, "Why on earth would you pass up on an opportunity like this?"

The answer is fear.

What are we so afraid of?

Fear plays a major role in the decisions that people make, especially when it comes to career choices. Fear in many ways can be so crippling that it not only can slow our progression, sometimes it stops us from progressing completely. For some, success and upward mobility are considered threatening or dangerous. This is because those types of changes put us in positions of visibility to be judged more heavily than we already are. And visibility in a lot of cases equates to vulnerability.

Going back to what we discussed earlier, when we feel vulnerable, we start to doubt ourselves. This self-doubt is far more deterring than the fear we have of others doubting us. It is as if we are afraid of our own success.

We are fearful that we will fail, and we fear that we will be judged.

Fear of Failure

For the women I spoke with in this study, fear of failure manifested itself by way of not wanting to be a disappointment to themselves and others. There was a constant questioning of whether or not they were good enough to do what was being asked of them, or could be asked of them. During my interview with Sandy K, fear of failure came up in this way:

> *"When I talked about how women are sometimes in their own way, it's just not so much as they're in their way, it's that it gets to the point where they get deterred. Is this going to be hard, or is this really for me? How much do I want to give up of myself or what I really want to do in order to make this happen? How*

important is that going to be?... What I've noticed is that when it comes to career trajectory, you have to be comfortable with selling yourself and being able to promote yourself to people who don't even know you."

Studies have shown that race and gender impact how fear is conceptualized. One study revealed that African American men and women are more prone to stressors, both chronic and acute, when it comes to institutionalized racism and discrimination. The same study also discovered that because African Americans have a stronger "external orientation," they are more likely to see their circumstances as being externally controlled and have a stronger belief in the control of powerful others.[24]

We place so much value on ourselves and our work, as we should, but there is a constant question as to whether or not others see the same potential in us. The unfortunate answer is that they usually don't. Because of this, we work extra hard to somehow try and meet unrealistic standards. In the backs of our minds, based on past experiences, we already know we won't be good enough in their eyes. The expectation that we will fail in the eyes of others causes us a great deal of stress; therefore, we often seek external validation that we usually won't receive. When we don't receive that validation, we begin to internalize what is truly a perceived failure, not an actual one.

Fear of Judgment

Fear of judgment was a prominent theme that emerged as well in the form of fear of outward judgment. Specifically by way of not taking actions to advance your career out of fear of not having the "right look."

As successful women of color, we are often the only ones in predominantly white spaces, and in almost all cases, subject to European beauty standards. Research has shown that these beauty standards are so ingrained in society that they have become institutionalized to the point where the decision a Black woman makes about how to style her hair can determine what kind of job she can get, have, and keep.[25]

When it comes to women of color, especially Black women, opinions about standards of beauty come from many angles. Most of these opinions come from the outside but in some cases, they come from the inside as well. Hair, makeup, clothing, and skin tone have historically been defining factors of beauty and success. The darker you are, the more barriers you'll face. Kinky hair will throw a kink in your chances of advancement.

Diana J was one woman I spoke to who lived with fear of judgment for quite some time during her career. There was an element of self-consciousness about her appearance and how others would judge her based on that appearance.

DIANA J'S STORY

Diana J is a proud Afro-Latina of Dominican descent. She is a first-generation American, and she identified her upbringing as playing a major role in many of the decisions she's made, both positive and negative. Here is what she shared:

"I think my childhood has been pretty much the bedrock of who I am, who I want to be, who I think I should be, and everything that deals with the self. The reason why I say this is because I was the first generation to be born here in the United States; [to this day] my mother still doesn't know English. Growing up, she was under public assistance and I would go with her. She would pull me from school, and we would go to welfare and I would be her interpreter. This is around 7 and 8, and the same way that I helped her, I would help a friend. I was always in a position where I had to ask or be involved in things that I necessarily should [should not have] been because of my age. In dealing with people with public assistance, in those offices, they have no windows, people are nasty and cranky.

"I [had] to explain to my mother what the lady was asking, then I had to explain what my mother was asking her. I was basically facilitating an adult conversation at the age of 8. That also molded me in the sense that I remember saying to myself, 'I never want to be on public assistance. I never want to be in anybody's office asking them for help. Never.' I went to my mother's jobs and I saw her work and I hated to see her friends crowding around the clock waiting for 15 minutes to pass, because they got paid by every quarter of the hour. I hated that feeling of clocking in or having someone or something dictate [my time].

"Those experiences shaped the person that I am. I was very determined to go to college. I didn't have any money, and I was quite naive as to how much money I did have. I had to figure out a way, when I first went to college, how to come up with $15,000 every semester. I made friends with financial aid people. I looked for scholarships. I did work-study. There was always a constant struggle or worry of the 'how?' I was going to pay for school. I had to worry about a lot of things that my friends didn't have to worry about. I remember being in college, walking around with holes in sneakers and not being able to easily replace them.

"I chose to move out of the dorm because it would be cheaper to have my own apartment, but then I had to deal with rent, food. Constantly having food, food shopping, juggling 2 jobs, and still maintaining a relatively good GPA. I always had to think about the future and be strategic.

> "I am a very driven person, but I'm also insecure. If there's an opportunity, like if I'm looking for a job for the next step of my career, there's a lot of times when I often question if I'm able to perform to the level of ... I have very high expectations of myself, very high expectations, so I always doubt my ability to do more. I always see myself as a simple person, and when I see other professionals regardless of what the packaging is, I do think about how is it, or why is it, or how come?"

It is clear that Diana is driven and has been able to persevere in spite of the challenges she faced growing up. However, there are still some insecurities. What should be noted is part of her last statement regarding how people are packaged. As we got further into our interview, Diana again mentioned "packaging" and how it is important for success.

When we talked about some of the barriers women of color face as they make the corporate climb, Diana mentioned how women are deterrents for other women, specifically as it relates to outward beauty. Diana even admitted that she, too, at times tries to conform to the beauty standards that are implied.

> "There have been certain situations I've been in, where at times [outward appearance] is a status symbol. What kind of purse you have, the shoes, it's materialistic. Appearance was more important than the quality of work the person was capable of doing. I'll be honest, I subscribe to that to an extent. If I have a presentation, I make sure that I'm better dressed that day. I wear makeup as a strategic tool. It's all part of your branding, or your packaging. I get that as well. I think when you make judgments based on how the person dresses and how the person puts together an outfit, it doesn't help anyone out."

Personally, I've always been taught to dress for the job you want, not the one you have. To some extent, I believe this is true, because as women of color, we are constantly being judged. Our outward appearance--skin color alone in most spaces--is an automatic dismissal. Because of this, we often must change who we are. Whether it is wearing makeup when we prefer to be natural, or muted tones even though bright colors give us energy. We are fearful of being who we are because we are always told we are not good enough. When we are not able to show up as our true selves, we won't be able to bring our "A" game.

LESSONS AND ADVICE

What lessons have we learned?

1. Fear is a B$%@& that will try to take you down every chance it gets. Getting to know your fears and tackling them before they can do you harm will only do you good.

2. There will always be someone somewhere who will judge you. The key is to not allow their judgment to dictate the actions you take to advance your career.

3. You will always be watched. Taking notice of who it is and why will allow you to make the appropriate adjustments if needed.

My advice...

Read this quote every morning when you wake up and every night before you go to sleep.

"Our deepest fear is not that we are inadequate. Our deepest fear is that we are powerful beyond measure. It is our light, not our darkness, that most frightens us. We ask ourselves 'Who am I to be brilliant, gorgeous, talented, fabulous?' Actually, who are you not to be?"- Marianne Williamson

Understand where your fears are coming from and realize that fear is a state. A state means that it can change. We can take steps toward removing our fears once we know what they are. We must not allow other people to project their fears onto us. To do this, we must recognize them for what they are.

Take pride in your gifts, share them with the world, and never compromise your values for the sake of someone else's comfort.

CHAPTER REFLECTION

Take a moment to reflect. Ask yourself...

- What are you afraid of?

- How do those fears impact your ability to move forward in your career?

- Do you ever question your potential and ability to be successful?

- If you've ever questioned yourself, do you believe these questions are prompted by external factors, or are they internal?

- Do you believe that others see the same potential and ability that you see in yourself?

- Do you believe that you are able to show up in the spaces you occupy as your authentic self?

- Have you ever felt that you had to change your preferred appearance in order to be accepted into certain spaces? Why or why not?

- When you've had to be unauthentic, or alter any part of yourself to be accepted into a space, were you able to perform at the level you know you are capable of?

- What are some ways you can get over the fears you have in relation to how you may be perceived or judged?

CHAPTER 8

Being Perfectly Imperfect

There is this idea that women must be perfect, and that they must do everything perfectly. What is not being realized, or even discussed, is where the definition of perfection came from. For a lot of women, if they don't feel that they can do something errorless, they will not do it at all. This is especially true for women of color. Failure for us, in any sense, has never been an option. Therefore, if there is the possibility of failure, we rarely, if ever, take a risk. What we fail to realize (pun intended), is that by not taking risks, we miss opportunities.

Preparation and Perfection

In early 2016, I attended a women's leadership development conference. In a session titled, "Don't Embrace Your Power, Embody It," one of the panel members asked the audience a question related to being prepared. She asked, "How much of the job does a woman need to know before she puts her hat in the ring?" An audience member shouted out "100 percent!" When asked how much of the job men needed to know, an audience member jokingly shouted "Zero!" The presenter then stated, "60 percent." Men only need to know 60 percent of the job before they will throw their hat in.

I am mentioning this because there is a notion of being prepared, or being unprepared, that seems to be a significant deterrent to leadership emergence of women of color. When you think about how women feel they must know 100 percent of the job before even considering putting themselves in a position to take advantage of it, one begs to question, should there be any wonder why there are so few women at the top? This belief of preparedness also leads back to the idea of perfection.

When I interviewed the women during my research, it was those who were considered early career who brought up preparedness the most. To some degree, there is an expectation that as they are in the early stages of their career, there would be some apprehension about lacking some skills and abilities. When you couple that with the lack of women of color available in leadership as role models, it can also be expected that there would be levels of self-consciousness and doubt about being successful in their current roles and in their aspirations for future roles.

What was surprising to me was the perspective of women who were well established in their careers. One particular quote that stood out came from Casandra R, an African American woman who was a media producer for an international organization. When the topic of preparedness came up, she stated:

> "I really go out of my way to prepare in advance of a meeting, to have done my homework ... kind of just like to prove yourself equal, that old saying."

While this is a very short statement, it spoke volumes. More specifically, the notion of proving oneself to be equal. From what was mentioned earlier, this statement says that this woman felt as if she had to come to a meeting with 100 percent of the knowledge of the material, compared to that of her male (often white) counterpart's 60 percent. What can be implied is that had she not felt like she was equally prepared, she may have not gone to the meeting, or she would not have put herself in a position to present and showcase her knowledge and talents.

Though the idea of preparedness seems like it may be different as one progresses in their career, it is still something that women of color face as deterrents and barriers. The notion that if you don't know everything, then you don't know enough and internalizing it prevents leadership emergence.

One thing that I don't believe many of us realize is that

focusing on trying to be perfect and do things perfectly can be detrimental to our health. I am a self-proclaimed perfectionist, but I am also a realist, so I have learned that perfection is relative. Like JC, the woman whose story I will share, I've suffered both mental and physical ailments due to the stress of trying to be perfect. I've also missed out on opportunities.

JC's STORY

JC is a young African American woman, a true millennial. I had the pleasure of working with and mentoring her for several years. She is the epitome of "Black girl magic," with so much drive, talent, and potential. Born and raised in New York City, JC is no stranger to hustle and bustle, moving fast, and being ready for whatever comes. JC was raised by her grandparents, so she's had a very different upbringing than most of her peers, especially when it comes to other women. There is a certain level of reserve that works both in her favor and against it.

At the time of our interview, JC worked for an international non-profit organization. A rising star at the time we met, she had already been promoted twice since she began working there. There were several themes that came out of my interview with her. The two most prevalent were fear and perfection. Primarily, she discussed fear in the form of self-doubt and fear of judgment. She stated:

> *"I don't like to make errors, so fear of error, making an error. When it comes to being a leader, that deters me from taking certain steps… I can be a pretty big realist in the idea that I know all humans are not perfect, or sometimes someone can suggest something for you, but you know how you are. I get a little bit of anxiety sometimes when it comes to just thinking. I'm a big thinker, so when it just comes to thinking about, 'Okay, you're going to read people. People are going to look up to you. They're going to watch everything you're doing.' Then I develop this anxiety where it*

could ... Even if it's stated plain on paper that, 'You should take this route,' I always think about the what if. It's just sometimes my thought process."

One of JC's biggest fears was being judged as incapable. As is evident in her words, a lot of this fear is internal. This goes back to the idea of needing to be perfect and being judged for not being perfect. JC provided an example that I thought emphasized this when we discussed opportunities and whether or not she takes advantage of them.

"Most of the opportunities that I have come across were brought to me. I have never been proactive, and I just think that comes from me being too self-aware, or unsure if I could do the job perfectly, because I am afraid of making mistakes, so that deters me. For example, when I was working at my last place of employment, I was a counselor and an assistant to the director for an after-school program. I was always a counselor, and I did my job to the best of my ability, and the director came to me one day and approached me about being his second-hand man in running the after-school program. I would have never approached him for that opportunity on my own."

JC went on to discuss how she believes women of color are viewed, stereotyped, generalized, and often compared to what is considered "perfection" when it comes to women in the workplace.

"I don't want to generalize, but I feel like when people look at women of color, they think of all the hardships we've been through. Because of this, we have to prove ourselves. When I say prove ourselves, meaning women of color, they tend to have the mindset, 'Oh, I can be like the white woman. I can have the knowledge that she has. I'm just as good.'"

To make the statement of "Oh, I can be like the white woman..." is problematic in several ways. One of the main reasons is that there are so few women of color in leadership positions that young women of color can look up to. Another is that we have been socialized to believe that we must use the "European standard" of everything as Polar North to compare ourselves to. For those of us already in positions of leadership, we have to be prepared to show our younger sisters that we are beacons for them, and that the only person they should compete with or compare themselves to is the former version of themselves.

The Imposter Syndrome

What JC and many of the other women profiled seem to suffer from is what is popularly termed the Imposter Syndrome or Imposter Phenomenon (IP). IP is generally associated with high achieving individuals. What often happens is that instead of having feelings of pride about their success, they "experience intense feelings of intellectual and/or professional fraudulence." These feelings are despite objective evidence that they have, in fact, made professional advancements and have received positive performance reviews, honors, and awards. Those who suffer from IP find it difficult, and sometimes impossible, to internalize their successes. They will often experience discrepancies between what they believe are others' perceptions of their success and their own perceptions as being deficient. [26]

Woah...

Let's take a step back and let that sink in. We work hard and make great achievements. Others acknowledge our achievements, yet we feel as if we either didn't really accomplish the things we've actually done, or believe we somehow only got to the positions we are in by fraudulent means. We tell ourselves we really aren't as smart as people think we are.

I am not going to lie, I have been a victim of IP. Why does this happen?

Early research has suggested that there are two main factors that contribute to IP, the first being family dynamics, and the second being societal sex-role stereotypes. Along with these factors, symptoms of IP include generalized anxiety, lack of self-confidence, depression, and frustration due to an inability to meet the standards of achievement we impose on ourselves.[27]

Does any of this sound familiar?

When you consider some of the earlier research from the 1970s, at the start of women having gained momentum in the workforce, in particular corporate America, there is no doubt that there would be a correlation between sex-role association and IP, which affects women more predominantly than men. IP happens when we are different from the majority of people we are around. If we are women among men, or people of color in predominantly white spaces, we will feel it the most. As women of color, we are a double minority, making us even more susceptible to IP than any other group.

Getting over IP is not an easy task, especially if you've been a high achiever all of your life. It's much more than just lacking confidence. When you lack self-confidence, you see a road block, accept that it is there, and don't move forward. With IP, you can create roadblocks for yourself. Because IP is about internalization, the roadblocks we create for ourselves are the most difficult to navigate.

LESSONS AND ADVICE

What lessons have we learned?

1. Trying to be perfect when perfect does not exist can kill your drive and desire to move forward.

2. It doesn't matter what you do or how great you do it; there will always be detractors. Don't let them dim your shine.

3. Always know that you are worthy of being in the spaces that you are in. Never feel as if you are not, and never let anyone tell you so.

My advice...

The dictionary definition of perfection is being as free as possible from all flaws or defects. What does that mean? Nothing and no one is perfect because, as humans, we are flawed. The only thing we can ever do is always do the best that we can and know that it is good enough.

Often, we are the smartest people in the room whether we've prepared ourselves to be in it or not. Take stock in that, and release some of the pressure you've put on yourself to be something that does not truly exist. Quiet the imposter. You've worked hard to be where you are and you deserve your seat at the table.

CHAPTER REFLECTION

Take a moment to reflect. Ask yourself...

- Have you ever felt the need to be "perfect"?

- How has the feeling of needing to perform perfectly impacted your ability to perform?

- Have you ever been praised for work you felt was not perfect? How did it make you feel?

- Where has the notion that you need to perform perfectly come from?

- Have you ever experienced Imposter Syndrome? If so, when, and in what context?

- Has Imposter Syndrome impacted your ability to to perform your job? If yes, how so?

- What activities can you engage in to help you get rid of Imposter Syndrome

CHAPTER 9

The Balancing Act

I am a firm believer that we are magical creatures with gifts beyond measure. With our collective power we can save the world. However, we cannot be Superwomen to everyone all the time!

Being Superwoman

Please be warned. The "Superwoman" complex, or schema as it is sometimes called, is very real and it can be detrimental to your health. Some studies suggest that there is a link between what is considered a "multiple role woman" and stress. In both popular culture and academic studies about women who have multiple roles within society, stress is often considered an inevitable outcome. In one particular study, stress has been defined as "a heightened state of emotional or physical arousal occurring when demands from the environment, such as engaging in multiple roles, place pressure on an individual's capacity to adapt."[28]

According to the American Psychological Association, the Sojourner Syndrome and the Superwoman Schema (SWS) concepts are used to explain the phenomenon of early onset of morbidity among African American women in response to persistent chronic stress and active coping associated with meeting day-to-day demands and having multiple caregiver roles."[29] When you put this into context, it appears we are being raised to kill ourselves literally and figuratively. Yes, that sounds very morose, but for some it has been their truth.

As women of color, our culture, norms, values, and history have taught us that we must be everything to everyone all the time, and we are expected to do so without any support. We are expected to be home taking care of our family (however defined), go to work, deal with racial and gender discrimination, be twice as good, work twice as hard, and be the epitome of health. It is impossible and we know it, so it is no wonder many of us shy away when it comes to taking on even more.

Culture and Multiple Roles

How we are brought up by our families and communities leaves a great impact on how we see the world and how we see ourselves. Our upbringing is what instills in us morals, values, and the expectations that we have of ourselves, our families, and society. Relationships within family and community are highly valued. This is evident in how women of color network. According to research, the support systems of African American women, where they exist, are mostly informal and consist of family, friends, and people within their community, e.g. churches and social clubs.[30]

Within the families and communities of women of color, family is above everything. Women are expected to take on certain roles to ensure the family is sustained. Because of these cultural expectations, women who are career focused often find themselves facing conflicts when their personal aspirations don't match what is deemed best for the family. These conflicts are often internal, by way of guilt, and can sometimes be external, by way of family turmoil. These conflicts can prevent women of color from emerging as leaders, as they may consciously choose not to take on certain roles to ensure they will meet family obligations and avoid conflict and feelings of guilt.

Role Expectations

The role of caretaker is one that all women are expected to accept; however, this is even more so in Asian, African American, and Latin American/Hispanic cultures. Several of the women I interviewed spoke of the roles they played or were expected to take on and the toll it has taken on their career advancement by either slowing it down or deterring it completely. Research has shown that women "work and comply with normative frameworks, even when it can be detrimental to themselves and other women."[31]

When asked about common barriers to leadership emergence that women face, one woman said:

> *"We believe that Black women are the souls of our families, our communities, our churches, our neighborhoods, our organizations, so therefore, we should be able to handle it all, do it all, be the leader of it all. We should be the CEO all the way down to the cook and the maid. Unfortunately, I believe particularly for women of color, we're more likely to overextend ourselves and undervalue our contribution. I know that may seem general to all women, but I think it's particularly true for Black women... We should be able to do everything. We should not speak up as much, we shouldn't complain because we can handle it, and I think that's something unique just to us, as Black women..."*

This expectation is one that can be linked to the time of slavery where slave women often felt the "brunt" of the load in having to work the fields or in the house, take care of their children and their master's children, and be there for their husbands, fathers, and/or brothers who were often carrying a burden of their own. This notion was captured by Zora Neale Hurston in her book "Their Eyes Were Watching God" when the character Nanny said:

> *"Honey, de white man is de ruler of everything as fur as Ah been able tuh find out. Maybe it's some place way off in de ocean where de Black man is in power, but we don't know nothin' but what we see. So de*

white man throw down de load and tell de nigger man tuh pick it up. He pick it up because he have to, but he don't tote it. He hand it to his womenfolks. De nigger woman is de mule uh de world so fur as Ah can see." (Hurston, 1990, pg. 17)[32]

While the character in the book refers to Black women as mules, what it implies is the work that they do. In so many ways, they carry everyone on their backs and do not get the credit, or relief, they deserve because this is the expectation. This expectation is what morphed into what is called the superwoman.

Family First

In conjunction with role expectations, the theme of family first also emerged. Specifically, the notion that family always comes before self. From an epistemological perspective, primarily in relation to cultural teachings, the cultures of people of color emphasize the whole, not the part. Thus, family is the unit, and as the teachings go, so must we.

One of the first women I interviewed, Giana K, was the first one to identify with putting family before self as a deterrent. She stated that it was not so much her family being the deterrent, but more so the role she had within the family and the implicit obligation to the family. She spoke of her role as a second mother to her siblings, which is often the case when you are the eldest and female. She also spoke about the struggle of removing herself from that role when it was no longer necessary.

GIANA K'S STORY

Giana K is a Pakistani American, devout Muslim, and the nicest person you will ever meet. She immigrated to the United States with her family when she was 14 years old. In Pakistan, she would have been considered as coming from a prestigious family that was steeped in tradition. There, the woman's work was tending to the husband, home, and children. When she came to the United States, the roles did not change; they grew. Here, her mom had to work, and so did she once she was old enough to get a job. And, as is tradition, being the eldest child and a girl, not only did she have the role of sibling, she played the role of mother when her own mother was away from the home.

During my interview with Giana, she spoke about the obstacles and deterrents she faced. While she believes they stemmed from within herself, and to some extent that was true, she also mentioned her role within her family and the responsibilities she had. She candidly stated that the prioritization of others over self, especially family, has been a deterrent for her and that it has become a habit that is difficult to break.

> *"I was ... I'm the oldest of the four siblings, so I always played a role of a second mother to my siblings, which I didn't necessarily need to. I guess it was the way I was brought up, taking better care of them and taking care of them before myself, so that kind of turned into a habit of putting myself to the side. Being selfless kind of contributed to that. I think it went to an extreme where even my siblings were like, no thank you, we don't need a second mother. That habit died very hard and I think it took me years to finally prioritize myself. I think women of color have priorities which may be different from the rest of the groups of women. I think ... and from my experience, and what I have observed is that women of color prioritize their families, their values, their cultures, and their traditional lifestyle more than anything else. They are very, very family oriented. I think in their case, their families also need to support them and align their own lifestyle with the success of their women, and not act as something which may serve as a barrier."*

Giana K went on to acknowledge the role she played in creating obstacles for herself, and how she always overextended herself.

> "I think my own biggest deterrent was my own personality of being over kind, over caring, over giving, but just not to myself to the degree where I had pretty much nothing left for myself. I wish that was something I would have worked on earlier in my life. I think had I done so earlier, I would have overcome these challenges sooner. It's never too late, I'm still working on it, and it's better to be late than never. I think it's my own state of mind because I can change my state of mind, I can change my thinking and set myself up for success or failure. I don't think any external factors are as strong in my case in my own state of mind, my own personality, my own lifestyle so to speak. I think if I had not done that (taken care of my siblings) for a long time, everybody would have been okay, maybe better, including me. I think that is something I have been working on for the past couple of years, more consciously and training myself to liberate myself from all those factors which are preventing me from moving forward."

Giana is one of a few people who realized earlier in her life and career (she's a millennial) that she needed to take a step back and consider that her family would have been okay if she had stopped playing the role of mother. She also acknowledged that she is a work in progress, and that it's never too late to change habitual behaviors, especially ones that are detrimental to her progression as a woman.

Because of expectations from their cultures, several of the women I interviewed had decided to prioritize their families over their careers. There is a contradictory notion that you cannot be the best at both having a career and taking care of your family; however, you are required to do so because you must be able to treat both with equal fervor.

Support

Family support, or the lack thereof, was prevalent among many of the women who spoke about the challenges of taking on multiple roles. They did not receive support in these two ways: first, support of family in allowing them to pursue their passion, and second, support of family in having a deeper understanding of the hard work it takes to grow professionally. Some of the women mentioned that while lack of family support was not necessarily a deterrent to their emergence as a leader, not having it posed multiple challenges. Family is often seen as the foundation of a person. When you don't have a foundation, or have one but it cannot comprehend the journey that you are on, movement can be difficult.

When considering the theme of support, overall, what was gathered was that a certain level of confidence is gained when you know you are not alone. Knowing that someone has your back, whether it is to give you a push as mentor, cheer you on as a peer, or keep you grounded as a family, you are more apt to take chances and be more confident. You can find balance.

I have struggled with many of the challenges these women have faced. There is a constant conflict of wanting to be there for your family, but also wishing to pursue your career goals. Like Giana, I was a second mother to my younger sibling partly because I actually needed to be, and partly because I thought I needed to be. While growing up, I saw the women in my family be Superwoman to everyone, so it became my Polar North. I have been blessed to have the support of my family throughout my leadership journey. While they may not have always understood some of the hardships that I have gone through, they have always been there and have given me an ear to vent to and a shoulder to cry on. They have also been ready to take a drive to wherever to stand up to who I felt had done me wrong. Many of us don't have that type of familial support, so, as a peer group, we need to fill that role and be there for each other.

LESSONS AND ADVICE

What lessons have we learned?

1. Trying to be Superwoman is not a realistic goal. Yes, many of us will take on multiple roles, but each one of us must remember that she is an individual. She cannot do everything at the same time, and that will be okay.

2. Sometimes you need to step away and know that everything will be okay, because most of the time it will be. Nothing in the world is more important than your health.

3. Sometimes you will not get the support you seek from others. People will not always understand your struggles or journey. They are not meant to, because it is YOUR journey.

My advice...

STOP trying to be the mother, wife, girlfriend, best friend, auntie, cousin, sister, work wife, leader, teacher, mentor, CEO, and sponsor to everyone and their momma. IT WILL KILL YOU!

While you may be an extraordinary human, you are still human, and you can break. We play many roles, wear many hats, and are important to many people. The most important thing to remember, however, is that we have to become important to ourselves.

Prioritize yourself and your health above all. Doing so will not make you any less of a mother, wife, sister, or CEO. It will make you a better one.

CHAPTER REFLECTION

Take a moment to reflect. Ask yourself...

- Are you or have you ever suffered from the Superwoman complex?

- What have been the implications (mental, physical, emotional) of trying to be Superwoman?

- Has your upbringing played a role in your perception of having to be Superwoman? How so?

- What steps can you take to break the habit of trying to do everything and be everyone to the people in your personal and professional life?

- What are some of the normative frameworks you feel you are expected to comply with?

- What role does or has your family played in excelling or deterring your professional advancement?

- Do you feel you have the support you need to reach your professional goals? What does or could that support look like?

PART FOUR

Investing in Ourselves and Each Other

"When you've worked hard, and done well, and walked through that doorway of opportunity, you do not slam it shut behind you. You reach back."

– MICHELLE OBAMA

CHAPTER 10

Making Connections and Creating Safe Spaces

Having a support system is critical for success. Where we may not have it at home, it is important to find it elsewhere. As professional women of color, we are often the only ones in the spaces we occupy outside of our homes. These include the office, the boardroom, even the coffee shop sometimes. Being the only person in these spaces creates a feeling of loneliness and isolation. You are not alone. There are women out there just like you seeking to be a part of a collective that will understand them and help them grow.

Making Connections

Finding the right people to connect with requires us to do things we may not be comfortable doing, such as networking. I hear it all the time: "I hate networking," or "networking is a waste of time." It is if you don't do it with intention. You have to look beyond the general conccpt of networking and view connecting with people as an investment in your social capital. Not only will you meet like-minded people, you can build a support network, generate clients, or meet potential business partners.

You have to also understand the importance of networking when it comes to advancing in your career. For women of color, this is especially true. Let's first look at it from the perspective of gender. Men generally have larger networks than women, and their networks are mostly comprised of colleagues, advisors, and friends. They take a strategic approach to building relationships. Conversely, women's networks tend to be comprised of familial and community relationships. This is considered the social approach. When we put networking in the context of organizations, because we as women are less strategic in how we network, we are at a greater disadvantage. As women of color, this is even more so.

The strategic approach to networking is just that. This approach employs a strategy with the specific end goal of gaining something that will improve your professional situation and advance your career. The social approach to networking is when you seek a group of individuals to simply connect with. There is no specific goal other than to get to know people. The social approach is generally the first step in making a connection with someone.

Let's not assume that the social approach to networking is a bad thing, because it is not. However, if your goal for networking is career promotion and advancement (which, as growing professionals it should be), you will need to take a strategic approach. Women often tend to have difficulties moving out of the social aspect of networking. If you consider the difficulties women have with accessing the necessary people to network with for career advancement in the first place, you can understand the difficulties in taking steps toward a strategic approach.

Once we are able to understand the true value of making connections, we can have a fuller understanding of its importance in being an effective leader. We will also be in a better position to foster connections between others. Having the ability to do this will bring tremendous value to the relationships you create.

Factors That Impact Our Ability to Connect Effectively

Recent research has found that ethnic minorities are at a disadvantage due to a lack of access or underutilization of professional networking. On the other hand, when considering ethnic minorities who do participate in professional networks, most people of color almost exclusively network within their own race.[33] Studies that have examined the differences in social capital from a racial perspective have revealed that African Americans not only face inequalities in social capital externally with other races such as whites, but also within their own race. Externally, one major difference in networks is that the networks that African Americans are part of tend to be informal and include family, friends, and people within their community, e.g. churches and social clubs. Internally, within Black communities, there is a hierarchy. While African Americans with both high and low socioeconomic status have access to the same networks, those in the lower class have a more difficult time obtaining access to more restricted groups which generally are those groups needed for advancement.[34]

As women of color, we are especially vulnerable to being held back from career advancement. This is because of the compounding factors of gender and race and the limitations presented due to limited access to and lesser use of professional networking.[35] The duality of race and gender in relation to African American women and networking and the implications networking has on career advancement pose several challenges. Race impacts our access to and our participation in formal networks. As minority women, our access to those who are in the right networks is tremendously limited and can impede our career advancement.[36]

What's Really Stopping Us?

Early in my research, I had the opportunity to connect with a few young women around networking to try and get a better sense as to why it's hard for us to connect with one another. Even amongst ourselves, we are afraid to connect out of fear that we will be judged by one another. For those early in their career, familiar themes emerged, specifically fear and negative self-perception. Our inability to connect with others on social and professional levels are significant barriers to our emergence as leaders and our career advancement.

It was mentioned earlier that even amongst ourselves there is a level of classism that shuts the doors of opportunity to some of our sisters. We have to do better. We, as a collective, are excluded from a multitude of spaces, which forces us to create our own.

Creating Safe Spaces

> *"Safe spaces aren't without fault, but they are vital environments that Black women must create to tell our stories outside of the white gaze."*
>
> – E. ALLMAN[37]

We live in a world where we are constantly undervalued and under-appreciated by most of the people we encounter on a daily basis. As women who face similar challenges, we should be able to be more empathetic with one another and create spaces where we can share our common goals and work together to find solutions to get through our challenges.

My personal connection journey started later in life, but as the saying goes, it's better late than never. I was one of those young women who was afraid to meet people out of fear that I would not be able to contribute anything of value to the conversation. Additionally, being in predominantly white organizations as a professional, my exposure to spaces that were created by and for women of color did not occur until later in my career.

Like many of you, I was one of those young women who steadily excelled in her career and saw fewer and fewer women like myself as I made my way into more senior roles. I felt alone. I had to do my own research to find out not only if there were groups, circles, and spaces where I could connect with other women of color, but also where to find them, and if they would accept me. I was lucky enough to find several. To my surprise, there were even whole conferences that were created just for us to network and connect with one another.

There is strength in numbers, so when we come together, work together, and build together, it makes it harder for mal-intended individuals to prevent us from making strides. There is also strength in community, and when we come together with shared goals, that is exactly what we become. When we have a sense of community, we are also more comfortable sharing our stories with, and seeking guidance from others.

LESSONS AND ADVICE

What lessons have we learned?

1. Connect with your sisters so that you are not alone. You'd be surprised that your experiences aren't as unique as you think.

2. Networking, when done correctly, can get you into the right doors and in front of the right people.

3. Create and join safe spaces meant for you and women like you. If we don't support each other, who will?

My advice...

Find a space that is right for you and your needs as an individual and professional. Find like-minded women who have already walked or are on the same path you are. The road to leadership is a lonely one, so having some company every now and again makes it less so. When you are among women who look like you, who have experienced what you've experienced, and who are open to supporting your growth, embrace them, no matter what their level or status is.

CHAPTER REFLECTION

Take a moment to reflect. Ask yourself...

- What are, if any, fears you have with connecting with people professionally?

- Have you been successful at connecting with the right people who can help you grow professionally?

- What approach have you used when networking, strategic, social, or both?

- What approach to networking have you found to be the most successful for you and why?

- Do you believe that if you changed your approach to networking that you would meet more, or better suited professional connections?

- What, if any, disadvantages do you feel as a woman of color when trying to make connections that will benefit you professionally?

- What, if anything, have you done to create safe spaces for women of color to connect and share their experiences?

- What do you think that we as a collective can do to better support one another?

CHAPTER 11

Developing Your Social Capital

Developing our social capital is making an investment in ourselves that can catapult the value of the connections that we make. Beyond networking for the purposes of our career advancement, the development of our social capital allows us to build connections that not only impact our careers, but the lives of those we work with and those whom we lead. It can also impact our lives outside of our work through the activities we engage in as supporters of our own professional development. When we mind shift from the size of our network to the value of the connections we have and our approach to creating and maintaining those connections, the connections we make become more meaningful, last longer, and bear endless fruit in the form of opportunity.

The Steps to Creating Value

As a concept, social capital is complex. Like leadership, there are several definitions. Each definition is dependent on the context within which it is studied. What seems to be a commonality between most of them are the associated dimensions of trust, norms, reciprocity, and networking association.[38] It may sound easy enough, but is anything ever that simple? Of course not. What makes it complex is the humans that play a role. As people, our interactions, how our interactions occur, when and with whom they occur, and the reason for the interactions are what determines our level of social capital.

Let's first review trust. As women of color, we are often slow to trust. In earlier chapters, we have talked about some of the reasons why that is. In some cases, it is because of our cultural upbringing. Trust, however, is the first step in building our social capital because it is the first step in building a relationship. Trust often occurs when we presume that someone engages in moral behavior, a key characteristic of leadership. When moral behavior is presumed, we can then begin to assess trust at varying levels. Take an inventory of your current level of trust. Is there a general sense of trust? Is there trust amongst and between the people you interact with the most (e.g. co-workers, colleagues, supervisors, working groups)? Who outside of your immediate team do you trust? What about organizational leadership? Once you have identified who you trust based on either a presumption or witness of moral behavior, you can take the first steps in building relationships.

Assuming you've developed trusting relationships, the next step in assessing your social capital is a review of your beliefs, assumptions, and experiences with reciprocity. The concept of reciprocity assumes two primary factors: (1) we should help those who help us, and (2) we should not cause any harm, reputational or otherwise, to those who have helped us. When you think about the exchanges you've had with others, have they been mutually beneficial? Have your exchanges resulted in useful advice or information, or any other potential or actual gains that will support your professional development? The answer should be yes. If it isn't, there should be a reconsideration of that particular relationship.

Now think about your level or participation in activities that will support your development. Social participation in professional activities is what will increase your network. This participation considers activities within and outside of your organization. Within the organization, consider the following:

- your participation in group work with members of your immediate team and/or other organizational working groups

- volunteering for special projects or stretch assignments

- participation in after-work activities with your colleagues; for example, going to happy hour or dinner
- engaging your colleagues in conversation about themselves--asking them how they've been, or about a vacation they just returned from
- appearing as a generally outgoing person and actively participating in group discussions or conversations
- Social participation outside of your organization can include activities like:
- joining professional groups. These can be specific to your profession or it can be an affinity group, for example, a group that caters to professional women of color that is not industry specific.
- attending conferences. This will put you in an environment with people who are seeking the same knowledge and growth you are.
- participating in communities of practice: (CoP)- a CoP is a group of individuals who share a common goal or passion, and who meet to exchange knowledge and learn collectively. For example, if you work in human resources, join an HR group.

Quality vs. Quantity

The components of your network are equally if not more important than how you develop it. Social capital considers several characteristics of your network when determining whether or not it is a quality network. While having a large network can be beneficial, if the connections you have are weak, how valuable can they be in helping you achieve your professional goals? On the other hand, weak connections or being acquainted with many people can lead to other stronger connections. What has to be considered, however, is the investment into these weaker connections, and if it is worth the time and effort.

When you assess your network, ask yourself the following questions:

- How large is my network?

- How far reaching is my network? Is it limited to people I work with? Outside of work, is it limited to people in my career field?

- Are those I network with only in my networks? Do they have connections outside of our shared connection?

- How frequently do I connect with those in my network?

- How long have I had relationships with the people in my network?

- How strong are the relationships with my connections? Do we connect on more than a superficial level? Do we have a personal or emotional connection? How available are they to me/how available am I to them?

When we think of the term capital, the word value should follow. In building your social capital, not only are you and the people in your network making an investment, you are getting stock in return. When you think about investments, you are considering the time you invest, the advice that you're able to provide, your access to resources, your ability to provide "safety" to those in your network, and the moral support you give. The same goes for the stock that you have. As you assess your level of stock, you should ask yourself:

- How much time have I had with people in my network?

- What useful (or helpful) advice have I been given?

- What is the level of access I have to my network? Is it priority access?

- Are the people in my network "safe"? Can I trust that there is confidentiality?

- Who in my network can provide moral support?

The value of your stock is the value of your social capital. Like with any investment, you want to have a diversified portfolio. Everyone in your network should not look like you. You should also be connected with people outside of your industry.

LESSONS AND ADVICE

What lessons have we learned?

1. There is an actual dollar value associated with your network. Investing your money wisely now will prove fruitful in the future.

2. The quality of the connections you have in your network is more important than the number of people you are connected with.

3. Others invest in you as you do them. The time, space, and energy you give others comes at a cost.

My advice...

Diversify your portfolio of connections. Invest in and take stock of the right people. If you are strategic about it, you will always get a return. Like with other financial investments, there are risks. What you have to consider is whether or not that risky investment will yield a return in the long run. To do this effectively, however, you have to plan your long-term goals.

CHAPTER REFLECTION

Take a moment to reflect. Ask yourself…

- What are the steps you take to build trusting relationships with your professional peers?

- What is your level of participation in professional activities outside of your organization or business?

- What type of activities do you engage in? Do these activities provide more value in their output than your investment in them?

- What professional groups, if any, do you belong to, and what is your level of return in comparison to your investment?

- What people resources do you need to advance yourself professionally?

- What knowledge resources do you need to advance yourself professionally?

- Are the networks you are in capable of providing you with the resources (people or knowledge) you need to advance yourself professionally?

CHAPTER 12

Become Your Sister's Keeper

It's hard enough for us to connect, but what seems to be even more difficult is to support one another.

What I found the most disheartening from my research was the fact that as women of color, we do not support each other. Several women expressed a feeling of disappointment, asking the question, "Since we share a common struggle, shouldn't we 'band together' and support each other so that we can all win, instead of competing with one another?" This specifically emerged from the theme of peer support. The women expressed a kind of surprise that this happens; however, there also seemed to be somewhat of an expectation that it might.

JC, one of the young women whose story we shared earlier, mentioned the lack of unity she witnessed among women of color. She said:

> "I feel like there's not enough unity, it's just competition amongst us, because we look the same, and I feel like we have a different view on who we are when we reach these leadership positions that we've worked so hard for."

As a follow-up, I asked her if she had any personal experiences where she felt there wasn't any unity, or if she felt that she was not being supported by a fellow woman of color. She shared the following:

> "I have [experienced barriers] in previous employment. It was explicitly stated, not to me, but to my other

coworkers, that the position that I received, the assistant director for the after-school program, another woman of color thought she would get it. It was just about, 'Oh, why did she get the job? [Me]. Why didn't I get that?' That's why I say competition. There is no ... 'Oh, congratulations. Girl, you did your thing,' or 'We both did our thing,' or 'Here's some ideas that can help this after-school program.' It was more so just a bitter communication that we had after that. That's an experience I've had with another woman of color who was going for the same position ... I wasn't even going for the position, but she was, and I happened to get it. It was more, 'I, I, I.' It wasn't, 'Oh, congratulations to you because it's good for us,' or 'It's good for the after-school program.'"

Another woman, Casandra N, the media producer you briefly met earlier in the book, shared her thoughts as well. She, too, mentioned her experience with competition among women of color, stating:

"I think there's still, even today, that competition thing that women won't band together ... which to me does not bear out."

She referenced her current employer, mentioning that her department is mostly women, yet there is no sisterhood, which seemed to be the expectation in an overall male dominated organization.

Divide and Conquer

We live in a male dominated society. As professional women of color, not only is it male dominated, it is predominantly white. We have been socialized to believe that we are beneath everyone else, and that if we ever want to be close to our white counterparts, we will have to screw over our fellow Black and brown colleagues. It's the house slave vs field slave situation. Unfortunately for some of us, this is the mentality that we have taken on. This is especially true for women.

When we engage in divisive behavior, we fail to realize how detrimental it is to us, as individuals, and for those who may be in line to follow in our footsteps. The truth is that there are such few opportunities for us to begin with. This is especially unfortunate, because according to the Center for American Progress, by the year 2030, there will be 83 million people entering the workforce, with nearly 30 percent of entrants being Hispanic, 13 percent Black, and 10 percent Asian, which will comprise more than 50 percent of the workforce. Additionally, the net growth of the workforce will be from people of color with the share of whites being in the negative over the next decade and people of color growing by 117 percent.[39]

Given that our numbers will be significantly higher and provide for more opportunity, it will be harder for others to divide us. What we have to keep in mind is that we have to stop being discordant amongst ourselves. The disconnect among and between us does not work in our favor. If anything, it not only slows our progression, and in some cases prevents it.

Lifting as You Climb

"Lifting as we climb" is the motto for the National Association of Colored Women's Clubs (NACWC). NACWC was founded in 1896 partly in response to the exclusion of many of the women's movements occurring during that time. Black women were not allowed into white women's spaces. Even though they fought for the same rights, as Black women they were seen as unequal. The NACWC was a place where Black women were able to support one another and work together to build a future for their communities. This included each other.

This motto has become the slogan for many of us women of color who have been given a hand, opportunity, space, mentorship, and sponsorship by a fellow woman of color once she rose through the ranks. When we bring each other up, we make ourselves stronger. We also provide support for one another. I asked the question earlier that it is lonely at the top for us, so why not have some company? When you are in a position to bring someone along with you and groom them, you are helping to create a colleague and possibly even a friend.

The Leadership Hierarchy

I want to take you back to an earlier chapter when we talked about the leadership hierarchy.[40] Here is what it looks like:

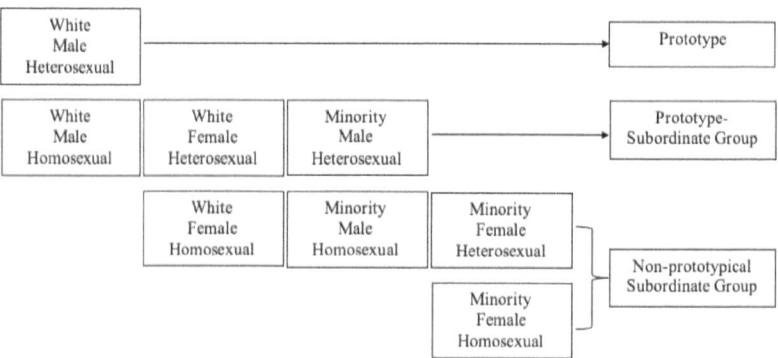

We, as women of color, are on the very bottom. Not only are we not considered the prototype of a leader, we aren't even considered to be a subordinate of the prototype. We are nonprototypical, which means that when people think of leaders, we are the last ones that come to mind.

When we think of the idea of having to climb a corporate ladder, from a purely conceptual lens, it is a process. There are at least six other groups that we have to surpass, seven if we are a woman of color who is a member of the LGBTQ community. So, yes, I can see why it may seem daunting to bring someone up along with you. But when you think about the fight you have to go through, why would you want to go through it alone? If you do go it alone, at the bare minimum, you'll want someone to celebrate your victory with you when you reach the top.

Paying it Forward

I am a proud member of the Black Women of Influence, a professional organization whose mission is "Helping Each Other Win." I will be honest, I did not know what that really meant until I was in a position to help other women of color win as professionals and leaders. In the next chapter, we will talk about mentors and sponsors, which are two very important roles we not only need to have in our lives, but we can support other women by serving in these roles. Until we are in positions to be mentors and sponsors, we should be partners. The best partner you can be is an accountability partner. You can hold each other accountable for your actions and behaviors, and promise to be there for one another regardless of who moves up first or fastest.

We need to be our sisters' keepers!

Being your sister's keeper means being responsible to her. It's helping create an environment that will allow her to develop and flourish. Putting her in check when she is getting out of hand, and being her shoulder to cry on when she is going through a hard time. Provide her with emotional support when she is working hard for that promotion, and congratulate her when she gets it. It's also reminding her that when she reaches the top, she should not forget about the other women just like her who will now embark on the same journey she has just completed.

> *"Leaders do not always have to transform people for them to flourish. Their greater responsibility is to create the social and material conditions under which people can and do flourish."*
>
> JOANNE CIULLA

LESSONS AND ADVICE

What lessons have we learned?

1. Be to others who you would want someone to be for you. Show up for someone, and someone will show up for you.

2. The only person you should be competing with is yourself. *"Nothing that is for you can be taken from you."* -Unknown

3. Being accountable for your sister helps you be accountable to yourself.

My advice...

There are too many people in the world who are against us, so we need to stop being against each other. Don't get me wrong; as I mentioned earlier, it doesn't matter what you do, you will always have detractors. Sometimes those detractors will be your own sister. What you can do is choose not to be a detractor for anyone. Pay it forward, offer your support, lift as you climb, and help other women of color win the way that you are.

CHAPTER REFLECTION

Take a moment to reflect. Ask yourself...

- What support have you received, if any, from other women of color in positions to help you grow professionally?

- Do you feel that women of color are doing a good job of supporting one another? Why or why not?

- What have you done, if anything, to support other women of color in achieving their professional goals?

- Do you feel like women of color engage in divisive activities when competing for leadership roles? Have you engaged in any divisive behavior?

- How can women of color better show up for each other?

- What specifically can we do to support one another in progressing professionally?

- How can we better be responsible to ourselves and women like us?

- Are there ways that we can collectively be more proactive in helping each other win? What can you do as an individual?

CHAPTER 13

Channeling Your Elders: Mentorship, Sponsorship, and your Virtual Board of Directors

If you are fortunate enough, at some point in your professional life you will have two types of people: a mentor and a sponsor. If you're even luckier, you will have nurtured enough valuable relationships to create your very own virtual board of directors. I'll explain what each of these are, what they can do for you, and why they are essential for your success as a leader, but first I want to talk about respecting your elders.

One of my absolute favorite books is called "The Little Black Book of Success: Laws of Leadership for Black Women."[41] At the end of each chapter, there are what the authors call "mammaisms." These "mammaisms" are sayings and phrases that, as a Black woman, you might hear one of the matriarchs in your family say. They are often words of advice or caution that will help you get past a challenge in your life. You heed those words because they come from someone who has experienced life challenges and survived. And, because they thought you special enough to share their stories with you, you showed them respect.

The same way we show our family elders respect, we should show our "professional elders" respect. It doesn't matter if they are in higher positions or subordinate ones. It doesn't matter if they work for you or you work for them. If they've been through it and are willing to drop some knowledge on you, shut up and listen.

Before I get into what mentoring is and what a mentor does, I want to emphasize the point I have made above. One of my greatest mentors was a woman named Michell. She worked for me for almost nine years and was my "right hand." She helped me build a department from the ground up. She was there when I went through personal ups and downs, as well as helped me through professional challenges. She provided me with some of the greatest professional advice I have ever received. People would ask, "How can she be your mentor when you are her boss?" My answer is, "She has had experiences that I have not yet had, and she has gotten through them; therefore, she has the knowledge to help me get through mine."

Mentors- Turning the Lights on for You

Mentoring or mentorship is defined as a mutually beneficial relationship that enhances the growth and advancement of both the mentor and mentee, where the mentor provides guidance and support to the mentee.

There are two types of mentoring:

1. **Psychosocial mentoring**: includes activities like role modeling, acceptance and confirmation, counseling, and friendship[42]
2. **Career mentoring**: includes activities and processes like sponsorship, coaching, protecting, and making the mentee known to others[43]

Research has shown that when mentoring is done effectively, it can be a catalyst for leadership advancement. When mentoring is considered excellent, it is believed that advancement to leadership occurs faster.

Scholars in the field of mentoring have identified three stages of a mentoring relationship:[44]

1. Initiation: During the initiation stage, the mentor establishes his/her competence and ability to provide support and guidance to the mentee.
2. Cultivation: The second stage is when the expectations of the mentee are tested against career functions and

psychosocial needs.

3. Separation: Finally, when the mentee has demonstrated his/her skills and is able to operate independently. At the end of the separation stage, the relationship between the mentor and mentee is redefined as a professional friendship.

There are several benefits to mentoring. Mary Pender Green LCSW-R, CGP, author of "Creative Membership and Career-Building Strategies,"[45] identifies specific benefits mentor and mentees received when in a mentoring relationship.

Some of the benefits for mentors include:
- gratification in fostering growth and helping others succeed
- the ability to delegate tasks (if the mentee works for you)
- gaining new insight and knowledge
- the ability to pass on knowledge and skills
- helping the mentee clarify her vision and goals

Benefits for the mentee include:

- developing a network of professionals in her field
- having access to skills, knowledge, and experiences beyond her years
- gaining organizational know-how
- having someone to confide in
- gaining opportunity for advancement
- gaining opportunities for increased visibility

Much of the literature on mentorship identifies the importance of mentorship in leadership emergence. Mentorship, within the context of an emerging theme from the research interviews, focused more on the idea of seeing and being around "someone like you." As a woman of color, being mentored by another woman of color, whether formally or informally, was important to them. According to some studies, this means that when your mentor looks like you, there is a higher likelihood that the relationship will be more fruitful than if it was with someone who doesn't.

Throughout the course of my interviews, several of the women mentioned lack of mentoring as a deterrent in their emergence as leaders. One young woman specifically mentioned that not having someone "like" her to look up to and seek advice from was a deterrent. She stated:

> *"There's only a handful of women who are minorities that I have to look up to, that I have to mentor me, and me as their mentee teach them something too, where there is a reciprocal relationship of knowledge and empowerment. That's also a deterrent for me, just because I don't have that exposure."*

This young woman mentioned that although she has been exposed to women of color who she would like to consider as mentors, there is a small number of those whom she could seek advice from.

In addition to a sense of comradery, having someone who can give you advice on how to navigate the workplace is also important. One of the women who could be considered an 'experienced professional' expressed this sentiment. She stated:

> *"I think that women who have [excelled] have had mentors, have had other leaders or women leaders or some other people in their lives who've kind of made out a pathway and shown them the things they [need] to enhance and do in order to really get to a certain level. I think women of color usually don't always have the mentorship that they need in order to do that. I also think that we don't always know the rules*

of the road, and I think it goes for all women, when it comes to negotiating a contract, when it comes to negotiating your salary, I think that you're at a loss because I don't think that you've been exposed in many ways, to how that is done in the workplace and how that's done in corporate America. I think that is really the biggest deterrent."

Elain D, a project manager at a private for-profit organization and the eldest participant in my research (65+), spoke about the things she felt she had missed out on throughout the course of her career because she did not have a role model. She expressed appreciation for seeing women of color move up the ranks within organizations because, as she moved throughout her career, seeing women of color in leadership were rare occurrences. Though this created a sense of pride, she stated that having a mentor to provide guidance and support would have boosted her confidence to pursue higher roles.

"There was one other thing I wanted ... for developing that confidence I needed, would be having either a mentor or a boss of some kind to be an advocate for [me] or an advocate for diversity, who really appreciated the point of view you bring versus having to be in a workplace where you feel a little bit on guard... or someone who would either want to promote your career or who was really interested in what you have to say. Those things, as well, would have helped me develop the confidence to see what leadership is like, to kind of be groomed for that. I think a lot of women miss out on that grooming to be a leader."

Confidence is a major factor in making decisions to take on certain responsibilities, especially the responsibility of managing the performance of a person, group of people, or an organization. Having someone in your corner to help you navigate the obstacles that come with being in a leadership role, or navigating the course to get you there, is necessary. When you are able to see someone who "made it," and that person can give you advice on how you can "make it too," the way in which you perceive your ability to be successful in a role that is already complicated without the compounding factors of gender and race is critical in determining a path forward.

There is often a certain level of comfort and relief when you have someone to share experiences with. Being able to seek the advice of someone who has walked the path you are currently on, and who has successfully reached their destination, helps develop a certain level of confidence. I was lucky enough early in my career to have women of color role models to look up to and to have as mentors. I would say, however, that I did not appreciate the value of those relationships when I had them. As I grew older and progressed in my career, I found it harder to navigate the road that I was on, and so I sought out new mentors. I still have those relationships today. Yes, I said relationships. You can and should have more than one mentor.

Scholars posit that women of color face the greatest barriers to accessing and utilizing mentoring relationships. This is partly due to having to navigate racism and sexism when seeking a mentor. Additionally, while mentoring can be used to promote success among underrepresented groups to higher ranks, women of color do not have access to the needed mentoring relationships.[46]

Sponsors - Keeping the Light On

Unlike a mentor who can provide you with advice on how to advance in your career, a sponsor is someone who can give you access to the people and resources needed to make that advancement happen. Sponsors are the ones who are actively advocating for you. Sponsors open the doors for you and vouch for your ability to be successful. Sponsors are often senior leaders within your organization or industry. They have a multitude of resources and extensive influence. Sponsors can also provide access to connections.

Some of what a sponsor does includes:[47]

- promoting you directly and using their influence and networks to connect you with stretch assignments, other senior leaders within the organization, and pay increases and promotions
- helping to drive your career vision
- giving you access to existing networks and helping to create new connections
- being vested in your upward movement
- using their platforms and reputation to champion your visibility
- involving you in experiences that enable your advancement

One of the best things a sponsor can do is add legitimacy to you and your work. When you are building a relationship with a sponsor, there must be a mutual level of respect, trust, and loyalty, because your sponsor is attaching his or her name to yours. If you fail, it will reflect poorly on them.

Sponsorship is pivotal for career success and leadership emergence. It's even more crucial for women, because we are half as likely to have a sponsor than our male counterparts. Like mentorship, sponsorship is especially challenging and elusive for women of color. These challenges make our ability to move upward very complex. A research study found that African American women executives not only have to work harder, they also outperform their counterparts, yet they are still excluded from informal social networks and have a harder time obtaining sponsors.[48]

As members from social groups that do not normally have access to leadership positions, you will find that we will frequently encounter a shift in our beliefs about whether or not we can be effective leaders. This is because we are often evaluated negatively regardless of our performance, which is the result of stereotyping. We are especially vulnerable before we even begin our journey toward organizational leadership. Because of things like stereotype threat, which we spoke about earlier, we tend to avoid leadership roles and settle for "nonthreatening" subordinate roles.[49] According to some reports, as racially/ethnically different women, we are more likely to downsize our aspirations as a consequence of exclusion. This is emphasized by the fact that we receive fewer promotions, are least likely to be mentored or sponsored by C-suite and senior executives, and because of this lack of mentoring and sponsorship, we are not given opportunities and access to career-advancing projects.[50]

Personal Virtual Board of Directors - Telling You When It's Time to Move to Another Room

We are the CEOs of our lives. Our lives are our businesses, and, like any well managed enterprise, we should have a solid group of advisors that can provide expertise in areas that we need expertise in. This will ensure that all of our bases are covered as we work toward building and maintaining our successes. This group of advisors is called a Virtual Personal Board of Directors (VPBOD).

Your VPBOD is your professional support network. They contain and have access to resources, knowledge, and expertise that you need to get ahead. This group is called a "virtual" board because they exist as a mental construct. What that means is you will not have actual in person meetings as a group, but they are individuals you can go to for advice. Your board members don't even have to know each other. They are, however, a trusted group of professionals who can serve as role models. Your VPBODs are people you can depend on to provide opinions and support that are unbiased, informed, and educated. They can also range from individuals whom you know personally, or those that are strictly professional connections.

Mary Pender Green, who we referenced earlier, says that you can see your VPBOD as a wagon wheel. You are the hub, and each board member is a spoke on the wheel. She explains that although you are moving together down the same road, you are at the center, and your VPBOD revolves around you. She identifies three characteristics of a VPBOD:

1. It's virtual- there are no formal meetings, members won't be aware of each other, and it is a means of organizing and

maintaining your professional development network.

2. It's personal- your VPBOD is people who you collect throughout your personal and professional journey. They help you meet your individual goals, even though they do not know they are on your board.

3. You choose your members- your VPBOD is made up of trusted advisors. They help you make important decisions about running your enterprise (your business, personal brand, career journey, etc.), and they are appointed by you.

Like any real board, the expectation is that you will have members who hold expertise in certain areas of life and career that will help you prosper. Here are some of what Mary Pender Green identifies as core positions.

- **The CEO** (You)
- **Chair of the Board**- the person you seek most often for advice
- **The Professional Guru-** someone that works in the same field as you, or may be considered a peer in title that can be a support and offer advice on professional questions that may be complicated
- **Chief Technology Officer-** someone who has technical expertise
- **Chief Financial Officer-** someone who has expertise in business or personal finance
- **Chief Political Analyst-** someone who is experienced in managing and working through office politics
- **Chief Legal Advisor-** someone well versed in the law (this person does not have to be an attorney; however, if they are, you will be better off)
- **The Ethics & Morals Officer-** someone that can guide you on issues that need the perspective of a moral or principled individual
- **Marketing & Branding Officer-** someone that can help

you develop your personal brand and advise you how to market yourself as a professional

- **Diversity and Equity Officer-** someone who can advise you on issues around organizational culture bias and discrimination. This person is also skilled at being able to provide you with an unbiased perspective on how you may be perceived by others.

- **The Education Officer-** someone that can advise you and be a resource for professional development and continuing education ideas

- **The Health and Wellness Expert-** someone that can assist you in managing the various health aspects of your life like your mental, physical, emotional, and spiritual health and the impact work may be having on them

Many of us have a VPBOD and don't realize it. Right now, they are just some really great people we know who can provide advice when it comes to certain aspects of our professional lives. This is what my situation was. Since learning of the VPBOD, I have begun to slot all my directors into their respective places at the table. Keep in mind that you may not have all these people in your life right now. I didn't. I gradually amassed them as I progressed as a professional.

It's important to note that you may be on a VPBOD and don't even know it. It's okay if you don't. What is important is that when you are sought after for your expertise, don't take the responsibility lightly. When people look to you to help them grow, it means that they trust you. It also means that you should trust yourself and what you are capable of doing.

LESSONS AND ADVICE

What lessons have we learned?

1. Navigating the road to professional success can be dark and lonely. Having a mentor, or someone who can "turn on the lights" for you, will be beneficial in the short and long run.

2. Everyone needs someone to talk about them when they aren't in the room. Your sponsor is your hype man. They get the crowd ready for your grand entrance.

3. You are a business, and all businesses that want to stay open have solid teams to make sure that business runs well at all times.

My advice...

You don't have to be on this journey alone. Seek out those who are smarter, wiser, and just as gifted if not more than you are. When you have a solid professional support system, whether they know they are supporting you or not, you can focus on yourself and your development. We don't know everything and, to be honest, we should not be expected to. When there is something you don't know, it's always good to have someone you can call. Just remember to also pick up the phone when someone calls you.

CHAPTER REFLECTION

Take a moment to reflect. Ask yourself...

- Who are or have been mentor(s) to you throughout your career?

- How did you build your relationships with your mentor(s)?

- What is the greatest thing you learned from your mentor? How have you carried that knowledge with you throughout your journey? How has that knowledge helped you grow?

- Are you a mentor to someone? How have you helped your mentee achieve success in their career?

- How has mentorship helped you in your leadership journey?

- Who is or has been a sponsor to you?

- How has that sponsorship helped you advance in your career?

- Beyond career advancement, what benefits have you found in having a sponsor?

- Do you have a virtual board of directors? Who is on your board and what role do they have?

- If you don't have a virtual board of directors, do you think you will benefit from having one? What will that benefit be?

PART FIVE

Being the Leaders We Were Meant to Be

"If people are doubting how far you can go, go so far that you can't hear them anymore."

– MICHELE RUIZ

CHAPTER 14

Becoming Who You Were Meant to Be

My research used a design called mixed methods. A mixed methods research design is an approach to research used in social, behavioral, and health sciences. It combines quantitative data that often reveals statistical trends, and qualitative data that is provided through stories and personal experiences.[51]

As a part of the quantitative phase of the research, 82 women completed a questionnaire and an assessment. I will share with you some of the results of the questionnaire, but first I want to provide you with some demographics of the participants.

Ethnicity

- 56% Black/African American
- 31% Latin American/Hispanic
- 6% Asian
- 6% Other
- 1% Pacific Islander

Highest Level of Education Completed

- 46% Master's Degree
- 39% Bachelor's Degree

- 10% Associates Degree
- 3% Doctoral Degree
- 2% Professional Degree (JD, MD)

Age

- 46% 26-34
- 35% 35-54
- 9% 18-25
- 9% 55-64
- 1% 65 and over

Job Function

- 23% Director
- 22% Coordinator
- 20% Manager
- 17% Consultant
- 12% Assistant
- 4% Chief Executive Officer
- 1% Executive VP
- 1% VP/Senior VP

Industry

- 34% Non-for-profit organization

- 30% Private for-profit organization
- 10% Local Government Agency
- 10% State Government Agency
- 6% Self-employed in own incorporated business, professional practice or firm
- 5% Self-employed in own not incorporated business, professional practice, or firm
- 4% Federal Government Agency

On the questionnaire, I presented the women with seven statements. These are three that I found to be the most revealing:

1. I identify myself as a leader
2. Others identify me as a leader
3. I believe I can be successful in a leadership role.

Ninety-eight percent of the women said they identified themselves as a leader. Ninety-six percent stated others identify them as a leader. And 98 percent stated they believe they can be successful in a leadership role.

We know we can be successful in anything we work hard for and put our mind to. We have the confidence in ourselves and know that others have confidence in us as well. All we have to do is set our plan into motion.

Leading Your Own Life

The women I spoke with during the qualitative phase of my research expressed what the quantitative results revealed. Several women, as they talked about their current journey, the challenges they've faced, and where they'd like to be in the future, saw the importance of taking their destiny into their own hands.

Giana K was the first to talk about taking the reins and leading one's own life. She talked about the natural transition from life leadership to leadership within the organization. It came down to taking control of what has an impact on your destiny and not allowing anyone else to have power over it.

> *"If you are essentially able to lead your own life, and the direction you are satisfied with, or in the direction you desire, then you can ... I think that you can lead others. First, if you're unable to lead your own life, or your own circumstances and find the solutions then you're not necessarily going to be very successful leading others."*

Casandra N, like Giana K, talked about taking ownership in the sense of knowing that there are things that are not within our individual control, like people's bias.

> *"There are some things you can control, and there are some things you cannot control. I think successful navigation is probably a combination of your determination to do what you want to do and doing it. I think any woman who really wants to be a leader, and really wants to go to corporate America can do it, but they may have to sacrifice some things. Having said that, I think that at the same time we have to be realistic... We don't have any control over someone else's bias, and I think performance can overcome that to a certain degree. .... You have no control over that, so you have to rely on experience, education, and the way that you approach it to overcome those things."*

Casandra N talked about identifying what she felt was realistic for her in trying to fight bias. However, what she learned was that you do not have control over what other people think of you, and that you cannot use that as an excuse. She found that focusing on what she could control, for example, her education, her approach to challenges, and what she took from the experiences she had are the most important.

Diana J was very direct in her statement that women of color fall prey to something that does not really exist. The "they" as she called it, explaining that "they" do not exist. It is only ourselves and what we do that define who we are and who we will become in life and work. She talked about how it is easier to blame someone or something for our own shortcomings, when, in reality, we are the controllers of our own destinies.

> *"I think that many times women get caught up with the emotion or the thought that someone is holding them down. I think it's more so because they haven't been able to properly self-diagnose their shortcomings.*
>
> *"I think a lot of women of color [fall prey to circumstances]. No one is holding us back. We are holding ourselves back. We define who it is that we are going to be, and we define how we're going to do the work. Once you identify who or what it is that you want to be about, work in those parameters."*

There are so many external factors that try and deter our emergence as leaders: sexism, racism, marginalization, unsupportive organizational environments, and so many more. While we have no control over them, we do have control over how we allow them to impact our growth as women and as professionals. We also have control over what we allow ourselves to accept and what we don't. I am a believer that we should never accept less than our very best selves, and we define who those people are.

LESSONS AND ADVICE

What lessons have we learned?

1. When you get to a place where you can accept the things that are not within your control and work on changing the things that you can, you will be in a much better mental and emotional space.

2. You have to know what you want to do before you go after it. Determination and a plan can work in your favor.

3. Only you can define the path you take and how you operate; no one else can do so.

My advice...

There will always be people, places, things, and situations that will try to deter you from taking that next step in life. You have to identify what is within your control to change. For those things that aren't, see them for what they are and move on. You can only control your own beliefs, thoughts, behaviors, and actions. As the saying goes, "If you believe it, you can achieve it." Believe in yourself and take action toward achieving your goals.

CHAPTER REFLECTION

Take a moment to reflect. Ask yourself...

- Do you feel that you are a leader within your life?

- What behaviors can you engage in to be more in control of your journey?

- What factors do you believe have an impact on your destiny? Which factors do you have control over?

- What is your process for identifying what is within and outside of your control?

- How do you move past detractors that are not within your control, that prevent your emergence as a leader?

- What does taking ownership of your journey look like? What do you feel are the required actions needed to get to the leadership position you want?

CHAPTER 15

Finding the HERO Within

Having the right attitude and right state of mind are the first steps in any journey that we decide to take. Whether it is asking for a promotion, negotiating a raise, applying for a new job, or taking the leap to become an entrepreneur, having a positive outlook on your ability to be successful at that endeavor is important. When we are in spaces that we feel do not consider our well-being as a priority, we must prioritize it ourselves.

One of the many areas of human capital development that I have learned throughout my doctoral studies, which I find to be critical in the success of any individual, whether it is in their personal or professional lives, is the concept of psychological capital (PsyCap).[52] Having its roots in positive psychology, PsyCap is an individual's positive psychological state of development that is characterized by:

Hope (H): the perseverance toward goals and, when necessary, the redirecting of the path to reach those goals in order to be successful

Efficacy (E): having confidence to take on and put in the necessary effort to succeed at challenging tasks

Resiliency (R): when faced with challenges and adversity, the ability to sustain and bounce back and beyond those challenges to attain success, and

Optimism (O): making a positive attribution about succeeding now and in the future

The HERO within.

While most of the research done on PsyCap has focused on individuals within an organizational context, the foundation of PsyCap can be adopted to individuals in their personal lives as well. Having a positive psychological state in every aspect of one's life is important in ensuring optimal functionality. Additionally, some research has shown that high levels of PsyCap positively influence overall well-being, health outcomes, lower cholesterol levels, lower body mass index (BMI), and higher satisfaction with relationships.

Hoping for the Best

We've all been told at some point in our lives that we should hope for the best, but prepare for the worst. I imagine many of us have even said it to ourselves. However, if one is truly hopeful, there will never be a corresponding expectation that whatever they are hoping for will not come to fruition. When we aspire to be or do anything, having hope is what will give us that kick-start to begin working toward realizing those aspirations.

Hope, when dissected, is a positive motivating state that is made up of two components: (1) goal-directed energy, and (2) planning toward goal achievement. Therefore, when we are hopeful or engage in the process of hopeful thinking, we put ourselves in a state of mind that allows us to become motivated to achieve our goals. There is a specific type of thinking that comes along with hope. It is called agency thinking. Agency thinking is our perceived capacity to use identified pathways to reach our desired goals. It involves engaging in positive self-talk, saying things to ourselves like "I can do this," or "I am unstoppable." Agency thinking is our motivation. This type of thinking is especially important when we are faced with roadblocks. It allows us to stay motivated and move forward with identifying alternatives.

When we are faced with adversity in our lives or in the workplace, it is important for us to remain hopeful. High levels of hope allow for us to think positively and therefore act positively. When we are hopeful, we are able to focus on our goals and make plans to achieve them. Hope allows us to recognize the options available to us, the ways in which we can obtain them, and plans for how to get there.

In the great words of Dr. Martin Luther King, *"We must accept finite disappointment but never lose infinite hope."*

When we are in environments that are not supportive to our growth, hope can be a guiding light. When we are hopeful that our goals are attainable, we are able to see how staying in unsupportive environments is preventing us from reaching them. If you ever find yourself in a state of mind of hopelessness, engaging in activities such as listing your goals, listing the barriers to those goals, and listing ways you can get around those barriers will shift your thinking and put you back on track.

Efficacious and Secure

Efficacy within the concept of PsyCap revolves around self-efficacy. Self-efficacy is the belief in our capability of producing a desired outcome. High levels of self-efficacy allow us to be confident in our abilities to exert control over our motivations, behaviors, and environments. This belief is a part of self-evaluation that can influence our experiences, our goals, how we work toward achieving them, the energy put into achieving our goals, and the likelihood that we will be successful.

Being in environments that constantly question our capabilities can easily cause us to doubt. Having high levels of self-efficacy makes quieting those doubtful voices (sometimes even our own) so much easier. When we become confident that we can take on the challenges presented to us, we start to put in the work to overcome them. How we feel, think, and what motivates us will change. The belief that we can get what we set out to obtain in and of itself incentivizes us to go and get it. The more we believe that we can achieve our goals, the harder we will work toward them, which will lead to a higher probability that we will be successful in attaining them.

When we are constantly faced with situations that challenge our ways of thinking about ourselves, our knowledge, our skills, our abilities, and our beliefs that we can make strides in our lives and careers become clouded. When we have low levels of self-efficacy, we tend to think negatively and become doubtful that we can achieve our goals or be successful in completing a project. We may avoid certain people or tasks, and we might only place ourselves in positions that we know or feel won't require us to work on a different level. [53]

Research has shown that when we do the following, our levels of self-efficacy increase:

1. **Focus on past successes**. Don't dwell on the negative. Focus on the times when you have been successful and model the steps that you took to get there. It's the concept of the law of attraction. What you put out into the universe is what you get back. Don't put emphasis on failures. Better yet, don't see anything as a failure; see it as a lesson learned on what not to do next time.

2. **Find others who are successful at what you want to do and model them**. While this may be a bit more challenging for us as women of color because there is so little representation at the top, we must find mentors. Seek out women who have successfully achieved their professional goals (or personal ones), ask them how they did it, and model their steps as it is applicable to your environment.

3. **Create situations for yourself that allow you to be successful**. Surround yourself with all of the things that will motivate you to work toward your goals. Stay away from, and do not engage in, negative actions. Find ways to discover an inner peace that will allow you to focus on the positive.

4. **Remove yourself from negative experiences and environments.** Yes, while we, as a group, are resilient (we will talk about that next), it does not mean that we have to stay in spaces that break us. Whenever possible, you have to rid yourself of people, places, and things that do not have your best interest in mind.

The way in which we perceive obstacles has an impact on how we overcome them. See the obstacles you face as steps closer to achieving your goal.

Resilient, Brilliant, and Strong

There are several definitions of resilience, yet when it comes to women of color, it can be defined as the ability to consistently overcome psychological, social, and emotional risks over an extended period of time. It is within your capabilities to understand the realities of the situations you are in and to think positively in situations of despair. It is within your capacities to find meaning when facing impossible situations. It is within your ability to improvise and deal with dire circumstances with whatever tools are at your disposal so that you can bounce back and find new ways to overcome them.

It is no secret that, as women of color, we must navigate multiple extremes. When it comes to the corporate environment, these specifically include navigating between extreme visibility and invisibility. We are either being watched in anticipation that we will make a mistake, or no one is paying attention to us because they believe we hold no real value. As resilient women, we are able to move past these challenges.

When you are faced with constant adversity, it is normal to feel defeated; however, you should never give up. Channel that inner voice of hope so that you can identify a pathway through the defeat. You can also work on developing these three key skills that will help you get into the right headspace to survive: (1) emotional intelligence, (2) authenticity, and (3) agility.[54]

Emotional intelligence has been shown to be extremely useful for individuals who frequently experience bias. Research around this topic identified that successful Black women walk a "tightrope of emotional expression." Because of the many stereotypes that exist, they have to develop an acute level of awareness regarding how they are perceived. They must also become skilled at stepping outside of themselves, so as to develop a different level of awareness.

Being authentic in spaces that want us to conform to a

certain set of standards or expectations can be challenging; nevertheless, authenticity in the face of adversity is important. Having a personal sense of self and connecting it with how you express yourself on the outside allows for a sense of peace. When it comes to leadership, authenticity is especially critical. For us, this means being able to align our racial and gender identities with the positions we hold. We can do this by finding roles that allow us to draw on our multiple identities to help ourselves and others achieve success.

Your ability to transform roadblocks and obstacles into opportunities is your agility. As a woman of color, I would venture to say you were born with this skill. Some of the women profiled in this book, who were first-generation Americans, who have grown up in the Jim Crow south, and have found their way to success, can be seen as testaments to this. You won't always encounter people or situations that "make sense," but your ability to be agile will allow you to turn those negative conditions into opportunities that will be beneficial for you.

Optimism in the Face of Uncertainty

Being positive about achieving success and reaching our goals is what optimism is all about. Believing that good things will happen, no matter what, puts us in a psychological state of mind that will keep us striving to do our best all of the time. Studies have shown that not only does optimism lead to better career success, it also leaves an impact on better social functioning.[55]

When we go back to the definition of leadership as being an exchange, high levels of social functionality are crucial to success. Levels of optimism are also associated with our ability to get through adverse situations and can aid in creating a psychological shift in thinking and behavior that allows us to be successful.

It has been evident throughout the course of this book that, as women, we fight an uphill battle. As women of color, not only is it uphill, there is rocky terrain, and there are boulders being tossed down onto us. Having a positive attributional style toward our ability to traverse that terrain makes getting to the top successfully, with minimum injuries, more highly probable.

LESSONS AND ADVICE

What lessons have we learned?

1. In the words of famed singer Lauren Hill, "How you gon' win when you ain't right within?" Having the right mindset about what your goals are and how you can achieve them will make them easier to achieve.

2. When we engage in positive thoughts and behaviors, the results we get will be positive.

3. Success is a mindset. When we believe that we are capable of doing and being anything that we want to be, we can achieve and become just that.

My advice...

Unleash the HERO within. Take responsibility for your resources by building them and using them to create the success you want for yourself. Don't rely on anyone else to validate what you already know about yourself. Know that the future belongs to you, and when in doubt, channel Proverbs 31:25:

> *"She is clothed with strength and dignity, and she laughs without fear of the future."*
>
> -PROVERBS 31:25

> *"She is clothed with strength and dignity, and she laughs without fear of the future."*
>
> -PROVERBS 31:25

CHAPTER REFLECTION

Take a moment to reflect. Ask yourself...

- Are you a hopeful person?

- How has hope played a role in your journey to become a leader?

- Do you believe that you are capable of achieving the goals you set for yourself?

- What factors impact your beliefs that you are capable of following through with the goals you set for yourself?

- Are you a resilient person? What experiences have played a role in developing your resilience to adversity?

- How can you transform roadblocks and obstacles into opportunities?

- Are you able to maintain a positive outlook when faced with challenges?

- How has maintaining a positive outlook helped you reach your goals?

CHAPTER 16

Stepping Out and Stepping In - Living Your Purpose

"When a man performs actions clinging blindly to his lower desires, then his actions bind him to the plane of ignorance...; but when the same actions are performed with surrender to God, they purify and liberate him."

-Isa Upanishads

For so long, as women of color, we have been socialized to believe that we are not worthy of anything other than what someone decides to give us. We constantly have to fight our way into spaces that we can provide value to, but do not see any value in us. We work hard for everyone, but often neglect ourselves. Though it may take some time, we do eventually rise. With the right support, and a deeper understanding of our environment and the people around us, we find ourselves, discover what we are meant to do, and step into our purposes.

I do not consider myself to be religious, but rather spiritual. I believe that there is a higher power that has led and continues to lead me to a higher calling. Though it can be interpreted in many ways, the scripture above, through my interpretation, has led me down a path that is clear and intentional. It has guided me into living my purpose, defining my success, and being fulfilled with my work.

In this chapter, I will share a piece of my story with you. I share it in hopes that it can inspire and guide you in finding and living your purpose and help you see the blessings that come along with doing so.

A Revelation

When it is finally revealed to you who you were meant to be, what you were meant to do, and whom you were meant to impact, it can be mind-blowing. It can also be quite frightening, especially when you realize that it has always been there, just hidden. We are good at hiding things such as our pain, our joy, our grief, our skills, abilities, talents, and the list goes on. Why do we hide them? Because we've been told by someone or something that we are either too much or not worth anything at all.

WE WEAR THE MASK

We wear the mask that grins and lies,

It hides our cheeks and shades our eyes,—

This debt we pay to human guile;

With torn and bleeding hearts we smile,

And mouth with myriad subtleties.

Why should the world be over-wise,

In counting all our tears and sighs?

Nay, let them only see us, while

We wear the mask.

We smile, but, O great Christ, our cries

To thee from tortured souls arise.

We sing, but oh the clay is vile

Beneath our feet, and long the mile;

But let the world dream otherwise,

We wear the mask!

This poem by Paul Laurence Dunbar is symbolic of what we, as women of color, face almost every day of our lives. We grin and bear when faced with microaggressions. We smile even though we are frustrated. We hide who we are and how we feel out of fear that, should we show people who we really are, we may be ostracized or discarded. In a world where this is the norm, what would we lose by taking the mask off? What would we lose by showing people who we really are? What would we lose by being authentic? What would we lose by opening ourselves to more than what others choose to give us?

We would lose absolutely nothing! What would happen is that we would actually gain more. We would gain clarity. We would gain closure. We would gain peace. We would gain freedom- the freedom to do, be, and serve who we were meant to.

My research is me without my mask. This book is me without my mask My story is me without my mask.

My Story

I am an African American woman born and raised in the Bronx, New York. I was raised in a single parent household by my mother, who was often supported by my grandmother. I come from a strong matriarchal family. My mother and grandmother worked tirelessly to take care of their families. They were my role models for what strong and independent looked like. To no surprise, like my mother and grandmother before me, I became Superwoman to everyone. Like them, and like the women I've interviewed during my research, until I discovered that I could be happy and successful, and that everyone would be okay if I stepped away, I nearly worked myself to death.

I am well educated. I have three degrees, the highest of them being a doctorate degree (Ph.D.) with a focus on human capital development. My career has been focused in the field of human resources, primarily in the public and not-for-profit sectors. Given my age (I'll never tell), the length of time I've been in my career, and which most recent positions I've held within organizations, I can be considered an executive. I have also embarked on an entrepreneurial journey as the CEO for a leadership development firm.

Though I've reached a certain level of success in my career, like many of the women I've met, and like many of you who are reading this book, I've faced barriers. The most prevalent barrier being racism. It did not matter where I worked, being a Black woman was always wrong. A close friend of mine would always joke that "I was the wrong color." While we'd laugh to keep ourselves from getting angry, I always reminded myself that I am who I was meant to be, and that the skin I am in only makes me better.

It took some time, but I finally took off the mask and began to love myself for who I really am: the authentic, unabashed, intelligent, beautiful, fiery, take no BS, mystical, magical, and unapologetic Black woman. When I discovered my purpose, I discovered myself, the person that had been hidden under the unrealistic expectations placed on her by everyone and everything, including herself.

Finding my Purpose

Purpose, by definition, is the reason we do what we do. For those of us who are blessed to find our purpose and be able to live in it, there is an understanding that the reason behind what we do is something beyond ourselves. We do the work we are called to do, not for superficial reasons, but to serve others in the way that our higher power has served us.

I discovered my purpose not too long ago, when I presented my first doctoral research paper at a conference. While I was initially reluctant to submit my proposal, a close friend made the convincing argument that in doing so, if I was selected, I would place myself in a better position as an academic, be more visible, have notoriety, etc. Unbeknownst to me at the time, the reason I should have been sharing my work was not so that people could know who I was, but so that my work could benefit others. As it turned out, it was. I met so many women (and men) who came to me and expressed how my work had spoken to them, and that what I had learned through my research and shared with them would help them better navigate the spaces they were in.

I did not know the true value of what I had created until I realized that I had not created it for myself. All the other things such as the accolades and name recognition came afterwards, and were secondary. To be quite honest, I realized it wasn't even something I cared about. Knowing that I had somehow changed someone's life in the slightest by sharing my knowledge and experience was far greater than anything I had imagined. I found out that I could create lasting change in others simply by sharing my story and the stories of women like me. I let go of wanting to do anything else in life. I had found my purpose.

Success

In finding my purpose, I have obtained a level of success I hadn't known existed. For me, success meant doing work that brought joy, knowledge, and insight to others. Since my first presentation, I have been continuously called to share my knowledge, inspire, and change the lives of so many women and girls. While my primary focus has been on the development of women and girls of color in the United States, my goal is to expand my work to include women and girls across the globe.

Through my personal work, affiliations, and partnerships, I have created a wider platform to reach a broader audience. I am now able to touch and change the lives of more people than I could have ever imagined. What I continue to marvel at is that I do not have to kill myself (literally or figuratively) to live my purpose and maintain my success. What I mean is that what I do is natural, and therefore it is effortless because it was a gift bestowed onto me. Because this is what I am called to do, not only can I do it effortlessly, I am rewarded every step of the way.

Living the Dream

One of my life's dreams is to find a platform where I could share my own story and the stories of women like me with the world. One of my other dreams is to become an author. I never thought that I could use my writing as the platform to achieve this, but here I am!

I do not propose that the road I have taken should be the same that you will take. It can't be. Your journey will be your own. I have been on this journey, and so have many other women, and, collectively, we can support each other along the way. It has taken some time for me to realize, but I was never on this journey alone, and neither are you. Find your sister friends. Walk beside one another. Share your stories, learn from one another, and pay it forward.

Optimizing Ourselves as Leaders

The traditional definition of optimization is to make the most effective use of a situation, opportunity, or resources. When we think of all of the situations, opportunities, and resources we have been given, the most effective way we can use them is by providing the same to others. I know that sounds a bit circular, and that's because it is. We optimize ourselves as people and as leaders by sharing what we have with others.

If you do a deep dive and think about the leadership model I mentioned in the introduction--Reflect, Invest, Optimize--it is never about just you as an individual. Self-reflection will always be primary because we have to think about ourselves, our lives, and our impact. However, who we are, how we live, and the impact we make will always affect those around us. As leaders, we have to constantly check ourselves to ensure we are in the right space and frame of mind to make lasting change.

If we don't invest in ourselves, who will? Taking the time to learn, grow, and improve ourselves as individuals helps us to become better leaders. Investing in ourselves occurs in various forms. This can be through continuing our education or taking time for ourselves to improve our mental health. We can also take time to curate our networks to ensure that time we spend cultivating relationships results in valuable ones. It goes back to the saying that we cannot take care of others if we cannot first take care of ourselves. Investing in ourselves, whether it is through our emotional, physical, or mental health or financially, is tantamount to ensuring continued success and progress in our endeavors.

What does it mean to optimize yourself as a leader? It means sharing your knowledge, skills, and abilities with others. It means passing it on and paying it forward. It means creating a legacy and making a positive impact on those around you. It means creating environments that will ensure our followers will flourish.

LESSONS AND ADVICE

What lessons have we learned?

1. Seeking to serve a purpose beyond yourself will yield for you abundantly.
2. Each one of us has a calling. Finding what that means for you will keep you fulfilled.
3. You define what success means for you. When you discover what it is, share your story so that others can be inspired to find out for themselves.

My advice...

Find your purpose. Work in your purpose. Live in your purpose. Do what fulfils you. Don't be afraid of who you are meant to become. Accept your past, live in the present, and look toward the future. I know that all sounds cliché, but it is the truth of so many women who have stepped into the purposeful lives they are living. We all have gifts to share with our communities and the world. Don't hide them. Share them.

CHAPTER REFLECTION

Take a moment to reflect. Ask yourself...

- Have I or do I wear a mask? Why do you feel the need to wear a mask?

- What would you lose by taking off the mask?

- What would you lose by showing people your authentic self?

- Have the stories of women like you helped you see the benefit in sharing your story with others?

- How can sharing your story benefit other women like you?

- What is your purpose?

- How can living in your purpose make your life better?

- How do you define success and what does success look like to you?

- How can you optimize yourself as a leader?

EPILOGUE

Though this is the end of the book, this is not the end of my journey. I have learned so much as I worked through and completed my research. While I sought to answer certain questions, many more came to light. In previous chapters, I mentioned that my research had two phases, one quantitative and the other qualitative. The qualitative piece is what bore much of the fruit for this book.

It helped answer the questions of:

1. What are the lived experiences of women of color in their journeys to attain leadership roles?

2. What are the internal and external factors that prevent women of color from attaining leadership roles/positions?

3. When presented with opportunities to serve in leadership roles, what are the reasons why women of color do not take advantage of them?

Lived Experiences

Studying the lived experiences of a group of people to identify a common concept or shared phenomenon is called phenomenology.[56] The phenomenon studied through my research was the leadership experience (emergence, development, and effectiveness) as experienced by women of color. What I found was that, overall, the experience of the women who participated were challenging ones; however, they were challenges that each woman felt she could and would take on.

Every woman I spoke with expressed experiencing some form of racism, sexism, and/or stereotype, either directly or indirectly, at some point throughout her life or career, which had made an impact on how she viewed herself and her abilities to be effective in leadership roles. Given the historic treatment of women, and people of color, these experiences would not seem uncommon.

I must say, I didn't think I'd be ready to hear the answers to the questions I posed, but I am glad I did because hearing those stories was the catalyst for this book. Not only did I learn about the lives of so many extraordinary women, I learned so much about myself and became curious about so many other things, including what my next steps could be.

Research Implications

Considering all I've learned, the final questions to be asked are: What does this all mean? What can we do to change this? How can we move in a direction where there is more ease, confidence, and choice by women of color to emerge as leaders?

From a research perspective, it is important to recognize the psychological barriers that prevent leadership emergence. Fear, low self-value, low self-worth, low self-esteem, and lack of confidence, to name a few. These barriers have a grave impact on how we think, behave, act, and, ultimately, how we perform in our personal and professional lives. Much of the research, both qualitative and quantitative, focuses on leadership traits and characteristics, but there is very little on the psychology behind leadership. As a researcher, one key question that I ask is: What level of psychological health is needed to be effective in leadership roles? Furthermore, I'd like to identify the impact that culture has on leadership emergence and the connection between the three.

From a psychological perspective, a review of the "self" and what impacts the "self" is needed. Notable psychologist Michael Argyle talks about four factors that influence the development of the self, with the "self" being inclusive of self-concept, self-image, self-esteem, self-worth, and the ideal self. The first factor is how others react to us. I would also include self-efficacy, which we talked about as a part of the HERO. The second, how we see ourselves in comparison to others. The third, what we are told and believe our social roles are. And fourth, how we identify with others. All of these factors are influenced by culture and societal views of individuals and groups as the society in which they live in has defined them. In relation to leadership emergence for women of color, these factors are very relevant because they help determine if a woman of color will emerge as a leader.

Diving a bit deeper, the impact of culture is multi-fold. First, research needs to identify culture at the individual level. How does the culture in which a person was reared impact their potential for professional development? Some research has already begun to look at social norms in relation to influence by stating that people most frequently look to social norms for a better understanding of how they should behave and respond to certain situations, predominantly in times of uncertainty. Considering women of color and the multitude of uncertainty they face, how they are being perceived, threats of stereotypes, and the uncertainty of navigating the corporate ladder, among others, understanding what their points of references are will provide deeper insight into the choices they make when faced with these uncertainties.

Second, a review of culture with respect to the philosophical differences that occur across varying cultures could be studied. How does culture on a philosophical level inform the decision-making processes, how relationships are built, and the expectations of individual behavior? In Chapter 2, I made reference to the work of Dr. Edwin Nichols, who developed the "Philosophical Aspects of Cultural Differences," which identifies the axiology, epistemology, logic, and process of individuals of different ethnic groups. Reviewing culture in relation to these philosophical realms may provide guidance on the approach for studying people of color in general, and women of color.

A CALL TO ACTION

Though the book has come to an end, this is not our final chapter. As we continue to work through the challenges we face daily to get to a point in our lives and careers where we can live in our purpose, I call on all of you to take action. I call on to you to share your story and show the world you are **#TheFaceOfLeadership**.

The movement has already begun and we have started taking over as business leaders and entrepreneurs. We have to maintain the momentum in opening and creating opportunities for ourselves and those coming up behind us. We can do this by not only being purposeful leaders, but responsible leaders. We have to shift from the idea of being responsible FOR people and move toward being responsible TO them.

RIO is the blueprint.

Reflect on your journey. Where have you come from? Where are you now? Where do you want to go?

Invest in yourself and the women around you. What do you need to get to a place of purpose? What resources do you have or need to secure in order to get you there?

Optimize yourself as a leader. Share your story and inspire other women like you. Who can you walk beside on their journey? What knowledge can you share? What resources can you give?

If you don't have a platform, don't worry. I will share mine with you.

Connect with me at info@waajidasmall.com. Let me be a resource for you. Let me help amplify your voice.

Share your story.

- Tell us who you are, what you do, where you are on your journey and where you want to go.

- How has or can this book help you?

- What lessons have you or are you learning on your leadership journey?

- Advice you can give the women walking alongside you and those just beginning their journey.

ACKNOWLEDGMENTS

Thank you to all of the women who have finished reading this book. You are on your journey toward leadership success, and now you know that you are not alone.

This book was a part of my own journey, and I am happy that I have reached one of my many destinations. This is a culmination of two years of research and two years of writing.

To my publisher, 13th & Joan, thank you for allowing me to join and contribute to the spaces you've created for women like me. My author coach, thank you for helping me make this book better!

To my draft copy editor, Elita Tzik Thomas, thank you for your diligence and patience.

Thank you to all of the young women who inspired me to write this book, the most passionate, driven, loyal women who I have been blessed to mentor: Ronette Wright, Emily Ramos, Sa'Dia Chance, Christine Stridiron, and Komal Gulzar. I love you all. You keep me young, humble, and grounded.

To my guru, Michell Andujar, you saved me in every sense of the word. You have been a mentor, confidante, cheerleader and friend.

Thank you to my dear friend, Moody Imam. You've read every single assignment and paper I've written during my doctoral research. Your feedback was invaluable... so was your grammar correction.

To my mentor, sponsor, and friend, Herman D. Smith, I would not be where I am in my career without your guidance and support.

To my sister and best friend, Shamika, I love you, baby girl. We are one. Thank you for always reminding me that focusing on myself is always top priority.

To my big brother, Jay, thank you for letting me practice being a boss every time you let me boss you around. The practice paid off... Look at me now!

To my other best friend and brother from another mother, Rakim, thank you for pushing me to be my greatest self through our imaginary competition. You may have more degrees, but I have a book!

To my baby brother, Bryant, thank you for being the first person to look up to me, and for showing me that I have so much to give to the world... Wakanda Forever!

Thank you to my academic mentors, Dr. Stephen Linenberger, Dr. John P. Fernandez, and Dr. Gregory Ashley. Without your guidance, I would not have been successful in completing my research.

To my amazing husband Christopher. Thank you for your love, encouragement and support. Our future daughters will be blessed to have a father who will stand beside them in all of their endeavors.

Biggest thank you to my mother, Pamela. Without you I would not be here. Thank you for birthing me, raising me to be the phenomenal woman I am, and for being my biggest protector.

To my grandmother, Ella, you are my earthly angel. You taught me to trust and have faith in God, and because of seeing your steadfast faith, mine has never wavered.

Finally, thank you to the man with many names, the Lord above, creator and master of the universe. I pray to you every night and thank you for holding my hand on journeys past, and ask that you continue to walk with me as I embark on future journeys. I can't wait to see where we go next.

30 DAY REFLECTION

My goal is to keep you motivated. One way to do this is to provide you with opportunities to continuously reflect. These reflections can be of your own words or through the words of others. Here are 30 quotes from influential women of color leaders who have and are making an impact in the world and on the lives of others. These words have kept me motivated and have allowed me to contemplate how I show up in every space that I enter. They also serve as a bit of daily motivation.

Read one quote each day for the next 30 days. As you contemplate the words of these phenomenal women, take a few notes on what these words mean to you, and how you can incorporate them into how you live, work, and interact with the world around you.

Day 1

"If you don't like something, change it. If you can't change it, change your attitude."

– MAYA ANGELOU

Day 2

"If you haven't forgiven yourself something, how can you forgive others?"

– Delores Huerta

Day 3

"An important attribute of success is to be yourself. Never hide what makes you, you."

– INDRA NOOYI

Day 4

"The only thing that separates women of colour from anyone else is opportunity."

– Viola Davis

Day 5

"If you want to do something, what does it matter where you are ranked? Nor does being a woman make a difference."

– Kalpana Chawla

Day 6

"It is not our differences that divide us. It is our inability to recognize, accept, and celebrate those differences."

– AUDRE LORDE

Day 7

"The most common way people give up their power is by thinking they don't have any."

– ALICE WALKER

Day 8

"When life hands you a difficult situation where you feel undervalued and disrespected, be bold and brave enough to know your worth."

– Yai Vargas

Day 9

"We're here for a reason. I believe a bit of the reason is to throw little torches out to lead people through the dark."

– WHOOPI GOLDBERG

Day 10

"Circumstances determined your past, the present is embracing you, and only you can define your future."

– TERESITA MARSAL-AVILA

Day 11

"Face challenges, fear, and frustration by seeking out knowledge and opportunities for growth."

– FANNY MAIRENA

Day 12

"You can't make decisions based on fear and the possibility of what might happen."

– MICHELLE OBAMA

Day 13

"Our life and our success will be measured by the quality of the life we lead and the lives we touch."

– SANDRA X PRADAS MARTIN

Day 14

"There's always something to suggest that you'll never be who you wanted to be. Your choice is to take it or keep on moving."

– PHYLICIA RASHAD

Day 15

"If I didn't define myself for myself, I would be crunched into other people's fantasies for me and eaten alive." -

– AUDRE LORDE

Day 16

"I don't have any time to stay up all night worrying about what someone who doesn't love me has to say about me."

— Viola Davis

Day 17

"Never be limited by other people's limited imaginations."

– Dr. Mae Jemison

Day 18

"Embrace your vulnerabilities, accept them, and forgive yourself."

– Angelica Monroy

Day 19

"You are no better than anyone else, and no one is better than you."

– Katherine Johnson

Day 20

"If you are fortunate to have opportunity, it is your duty to make sure other people have those opportunities as well."

– Kamala Harris

Day 21

"Sisters are more than the sum of their relative disadvantages: They are active against agents who craft meaning out of their circumstances and do so in complicated and diverse ways."

– MELISSA HARRIS-PERRY

Day 22

"If I made it, it's because I was game enough to take a lot of punishment along the way and half because there were a lot of people who cared enough to help me."

– ALTHEA GIBSON

Day 23

"Just remember that your real job is that if you are free, you need to free somebody else. If you have some power, then your job is to empower somebody else."

– Toni Morrison

Day 24

"To bring about change, you must not be afraid to take the first step. We will fail when we fail to try."

– ROSA PARKS

Day 25

"Every time you state what you want or believe, you're the first to hear it. It's a message to both you and others about what you think is possible. Don't put a ceiling on yourself."

– OPRAH WINFREY

Day 26

"Strive to be a person of value, and success will undeniably follow."

– NENCI RODRIGUEZ

Day 27

"You never know which experiences of life are going to be of value . . . You've got to leave yourself open to the hidden opportunities."

– ROBIN ROBERTS

Day 28

"Every great dream begins with a dreamer. Always remember, you have within you the strength, the patience, and the passion to reach for the stars to change the world."

– HARRIET TUBMAN

Day 29

"When I use my strength in the service of my vision it makes no difference whether or not I am afraid."

– AUDRE LORDE

Day 30

"What's the world for if you can't make it up the way you want it?"

– TONI MORRISON

APPENDIX A

SAMPLE INTERVIEW PROTOCOL

1. How would you define a leader?

2. Based on your definition of a leader, would you consider yourself a leader? Why/Why not?

3. How would you describe yourself as a leader, e.g. your style, expectations of those you lead, and your values?

4. How do you think other people will view/view you as a leader? How would they describe your style of leadership and your values as a leader?

5. There are certain traits that are said to be associated with leadership. The most common are the Big 5 (Openness, Conscientiousness, Extraversion, Agreeableness, Neuroticism). Do you believe you possess these traits? Where would you say you fare the strongest and weakest, and why?

6. Research has shown that both internal and external factors play a role in leadership emergence and effectiveness. The internal factors being traits and the external factors being environmental. What external factors would you say will play/have played a role in your emergence as a leader or deterrence as a leader, and why?

7. If presented with an opportunity to take on a leadership role, would you be proactive in volunteering for it? Why/why not? (Early Career: 1-7 years of work experience with or without having the responsibility of leading people)

8. Have you ever been presented with an opportunity to take on a leadership role? If yes, were you proactive in

volunteering to take on the role? Why/Why not? (Emerging Leader: 8-15 years of experience and having/having had the responsibility of leading people)

9. Thinking about the course of your career and various leadership roles you have held, were all of them opportunities? How did you obtain these roles? Did you volunteer (raise your hand) or were you appointed? For those opportunities that you did not raise your hand for, why didn't you? (Existing Leader: 15+ years of experience and having/having had the responsibility of leading people)

10. What, if any, do you feel are barriers that women experience in their ascent to leadership?

11. With the knowledge that you have the traits that have been identified as predictors of leadership emergence and effectiveness (meaning you have what it takes to be a good leader), what would you say have been/would be/are the biggest deterrents that would prevent you from actively seeking out leadership roles?

12. Of these barriers, what do you believe are the most commonly experienced among all women, and why?

13. Which, if any, do you feel are the most commonly experienced by women of color, and why?

TABLES

Description of Levels of Leadership

Level of Leadership	Definition
Early Career	Having 0-7 years of work experience with or without the responsibility of leading individuals or groups/teams in completing daily tasks or projects/assignments.
Emerging Leader	8-15 years of work experience with the responsibility of leading individuals or groups/teams in completing daily tasks or projects/assignments.
Experienced Leader	15 or more years of work experience with the responsibility of leading individuals or groups/teams in completing daily tasks or projects/assignments

APPENDIX B

Research Participant Demographics and Questionnaire Results

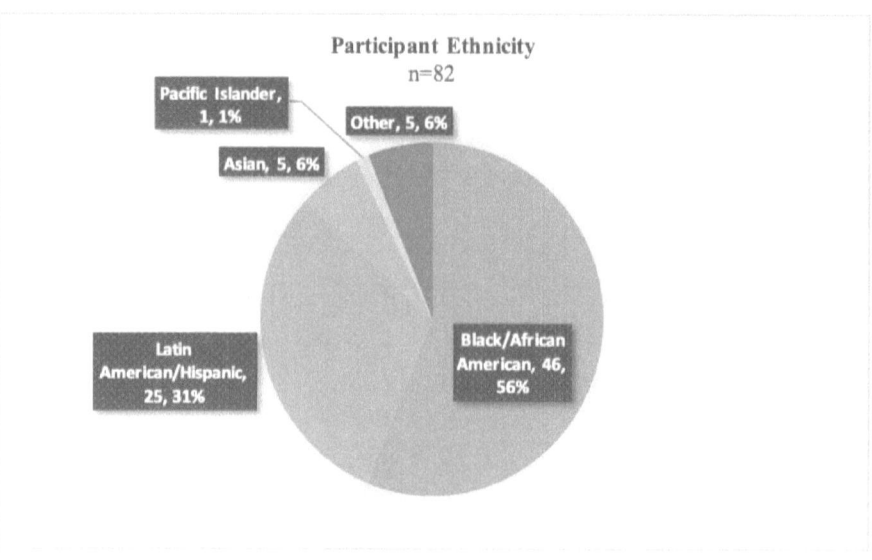

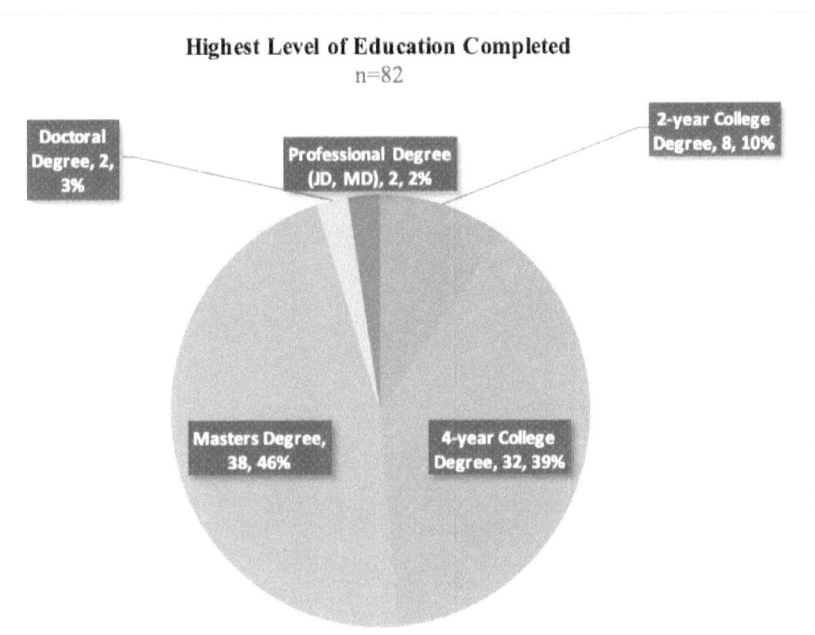

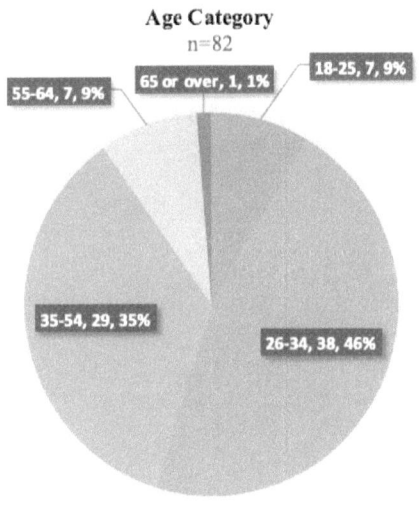

OUR LEADERSHIP JOURNEY

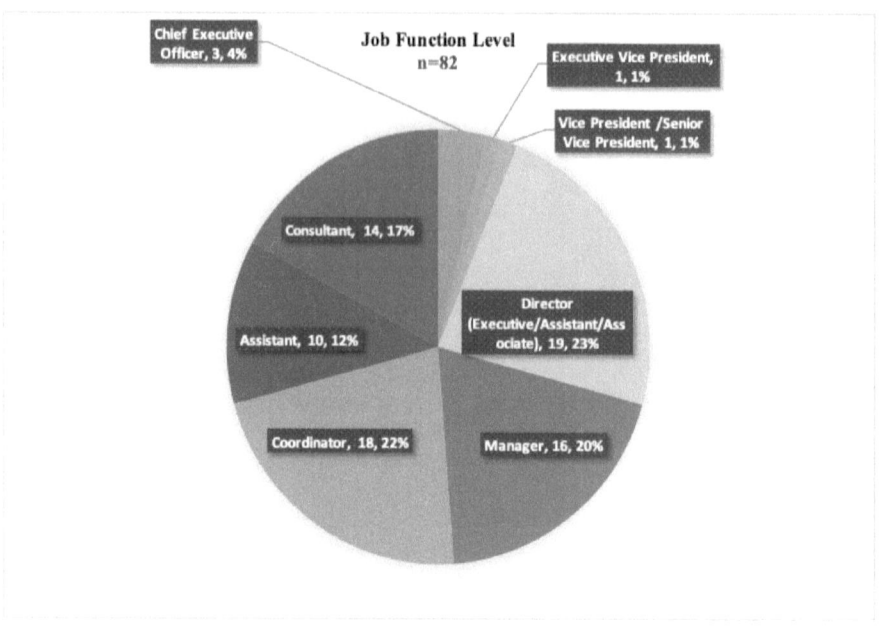

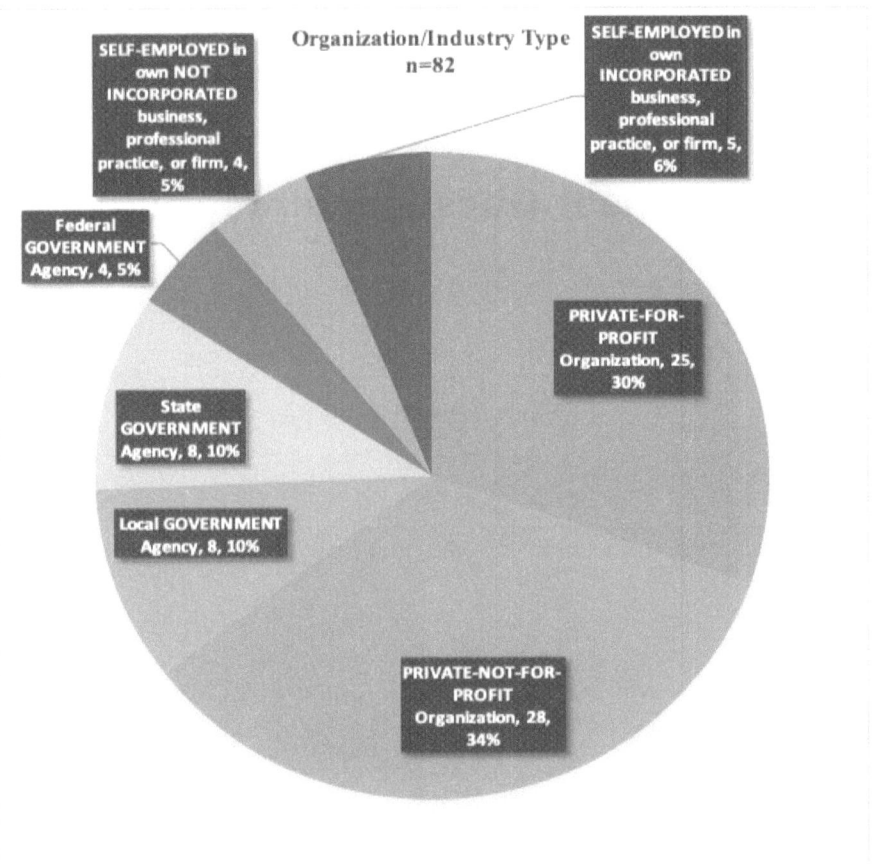

APPENDIX C

Participant Questionnaire Results

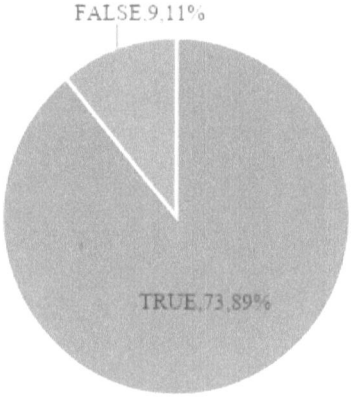

Others Identify me as a leader.

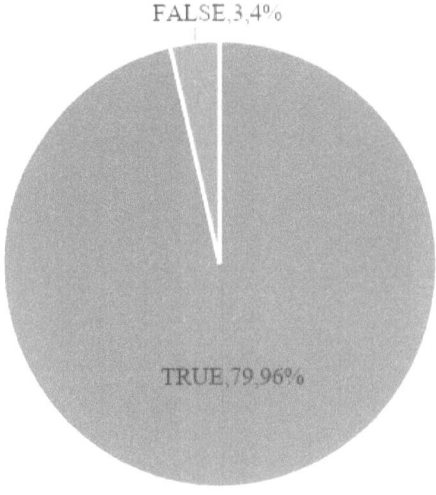

When presented with opportunities to lead, I place myself in a position to take advantage of them.

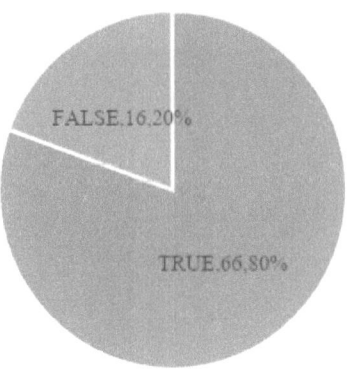

OUR LEADERSHIP JOURNEY

I do not actively seek opportunities to lead.

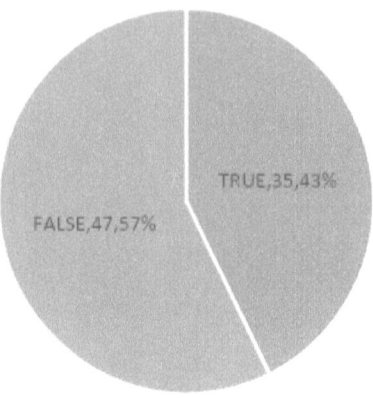

I believe I can be successful in a leadership role.

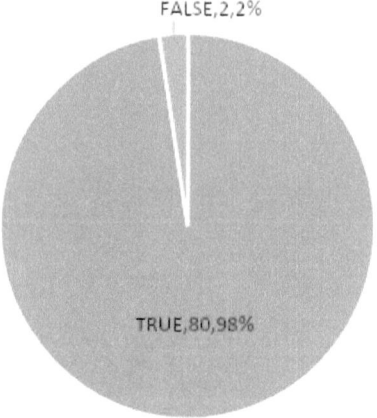

I believe I possess the characteristics to be a good leader.

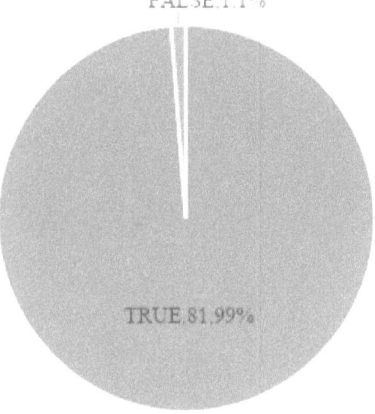

I seek out opportunities that will allow me to showcase my ability to lead.

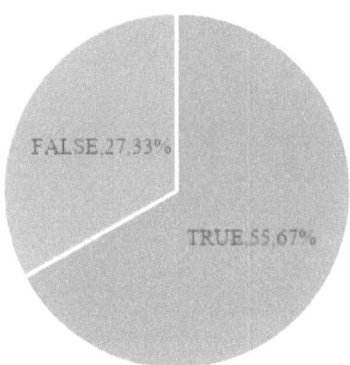

ENDNOTES

1. Mittal, R. and Elias, S. (2016). Social power and leadership in cross cultural context. Journal of Management Development 35 (1) pp. 58-74

2. House, R.J., Hanges, P.J., Javidian, M., Dorgman, P.W., and Gupta, V., GLOBE Associates (2004), Leadership, Culture and Organizations: The GLOBE Study of 62 Societies, Sage Publications Inc., Thousand Oaks, CA.

3. a. Ciulla, J. B. (2011). Handmaiden and queen: what philosophers find in the question: "What is a leader?" In M. Harvey & R. E. Riggio (Eds.), Leadership studies: The dialog of disciplines (pp. 54– 63)

   b. Garrick, L.E. (2006). 500 years of leadership theory: The challenge of learning to lead. NorthShore Group.

   c. Hogan, R., & Kaiser, R. B. (2005). What we know about leadership. Review of General Psychology, 9(2), 169-180.

   d. Kilburg, R. R., & Donohue, M. D. (2011). Toward a "grand unifying theory" of leadership: Implications for consulting psychology. Consulting Psychology Journal: Practice and Research, 63(1), 6-25.

4. Heere, B., Walker, M., Gibson, H., Thapa, B., Geldenhuys, S., & Coetzee, W. (2014). Questioning the validity of race as a social construct: Examining race and ethnicity in the 'rainbow nation'. African Social Science Review, 7(1)

5. a. Purdie-Vaughns, V., & Eibach, R. P. (2008). Intersectional invisibility: The distinctive advantages and disadvantages of multiple subordinate-group identities. Sex Roles, 59(5-6), 377-391.

b. Sanchez-Hucles, J., & Davis, D. D. (2010). Women and women of color in leadership: Complexity, identity, and intersectionality. The American Psychologist, 65(3), 171.

6. Nichols, E. (1976). The Philosophical Aspects of Cultural Differences. Unpublished manuscript presented at the meeting of the World Psychiatric Association, Ibadan, Nigeria, Nov. 1976.

7. Dr. Nichols' original ethnic categories identified Native Americans as a separate group. The adapted version of his work includes Native Americans among Asians, Asian Americans and Polynesians, removes Arabs and identifies Mediterranean and Middle Eastern in place of this based on shared worldviews. This Is the best adaptation based on the current U.S. categorizations. (source: Afrometaphysiscs.org)

8. Stanford Encyclopedia of Philosophy. http://plato.stanford.edu/entries/epistemology/

9. Fernandez, John P. (2013). Leading in a Diverse and Conflicted World: Crucial Lessons for the 21st Century.

10. Older workers are defined as 50 years of age or older per the CDC Older Employees in the Workforce Brief. https://www.cdc.gov/workplacehealthpromotion/tools-resources/pdfs/Issue_Brief_No_1_Older_Employees_in_the_Workplace_7-12-2012_FINAL508_1.pdf

11. Catalyst. (2014). Feeling different: Being the "Other" in US workplaces. Retrieved from http://www.catalyst.org/system/files/feeling_different_being_the_other_in_us_workplaces.pdf

12. Vuong, A. (October 25, 2013). The Role of People of Color in the Future Workforce. Center for American Progress Blog. Retrieved from https://www.americanprogress.org/issues/immigration/news/2013/10/25/77924/the-role-of-people-of-color-in-the-future-workforce

13. Vardiman, P. D., Houghton, J. D., & Jinkerson, D. L. (2006). Environmental leadership development: Toward a contextual model of leader selection and effectiveness. Leadership & Organization Development Journal, 27(1), 93-105.

14. Yukl, G., Gordon, A., & Taber, T. (2002). A hierarchical taxonomy of leadership behavior: Integrating a half century of behavior research. Journal of Leadership & Organizational Studies, 9(1), 15-32.

15. Kim, S. (2013). Networking enablers, constraints and dynamics: A qualitative analysis. Career Development International, 18(2), 120-138.

16. Reynolds-Dobbs, W., Thomas, K. M., & Harrison, M. S. (2008). From mammy to superwoman. Images that hinder Black women's career development. Journal of Career Development, 35(2), 129-150. doi:http://dx.doi.org/10.1177/0894845308325645

17. Sanchez-Hucles, J., & Davis, D. D. (2010). Women and women of color in leadership: Complexity, identity, and intersectionality. The American Psychologist, 65(3), 171.

18. Cook, A., & Glass, C. (2014a). Above the glass ceiling: When are women and racial/ethnic minorities promoted to CEO? Strategic Management Journal, 35(7), 1080. Cook, A., & Glass, C. (2014b). Women and top leadership positions: Towards an institutional analysis. Gender, Work and Organization, 21(1), 91-103.

19. Eagly, A. H., & Chin, J. L. (2010). Diversity and leadership in a changing world. The American Psychologist, 65(3), 216.

20. a. Carton, A. M., & Rosette, A. S. (2011). Explaining bias against Black leaders: integrating theory on information processing and goal-based stereotyping. Academy of Management Journal, 54(6), 1141.

    b. Davies, P. G., Spencer, S. J., & Steele, C. M. (2005). Clearing the air: Identity safety moderates the effects of stereotype threat on women's leadership aspirations. Journal of Personality and Social Psychology, 88(2), 276-287.

21. Kowalski, J. (2009). Stereotypes of History: Reconstructing Truth and the Black Mammy. transcending silence. Retrieved from https://www.albany.edu/womensstudies/journal/2009/kowalski/kowalski.html

22. Jones, T. & Norwood K. (2017). Aggressive encounters & white fragility: Deconstructing the trope of the Angry Black Woman. Iowa Law Review 102(5). Retrieved from https://ilr.law.uiowa.edu/assets/Uploads/ILR-102-5-Jones.pdf

23. Adolphs, R. (2013). The Biology of Fear. Current Biology: CB, 23(2), R79–R93. http://doi.org/10.1016/j.cub.2012.11.055

24. Muroff, J., Spencer, M. S., Ross, A. M., Williams, D. R., Neighbors, H. W., & Jackson, J. S. (2014). Race, Gender, and Conceptualizations of Fear. Professional psychology, research and practice, 45(3), 153-162.

25. King, V. & Niably, D. (2013). The politics of Black womens' hair. Journal of Undergraduate Research at Minnesota State University, Mankato, 13(4). Retrieved from https://cornerstone.lib.mnsu.edu/cgi/viewcontent.cgi?referer=https://www.google.com/&httpsredir=1&article=1003&context=jur

26. Neureiter, M., & Traut-Mattausch, E. (2016). Inspecting the Dangers of Feeling like a Fake: An Empirical Investigation of the Impostor Phenomenon in the World of Work. Frontiers in psychology, 7, 1445. doi:10.3389/fpsyg.2016.01445

27. Clance, R., Imes, P., P & Ament Imes, S. (1978). The imposter phenomenon in high achieving women: Dynamics and therapeutic intervention. Psychotherapy: Theory, Research & Practice. 15. 241-247. 10.1037/h0086006.

28. Sumra, M. K., & Schillaci, M. A. (2015). Stress and the Multiple-Role Woman: Taking a Closer Look at the "Superwoman." PLoS ONE, 10(3), e0120952. http://doi.org/10.1371/journal.pone.0120952.

29. The American Psychological Association (2018). Fact Sheet: Health Disparities and Stress. Retreived from http://www.apa.org/topics/health-disparities/fact-sheet-stress.aspx

30. Reid, A. (2010). The political implication of social capital. Harvard Journal of African American Public Policy, 16, 3-19.

31. Mavin, S. & Grandy, G. (2016). A theory of abject appearance: Women elite leaders' intra-gender 'management' of bodies and appearance. Human Relations, published online before print January 7, 2016, doi: 10.1177/0018726715609107. Retrieved from http://hum.sagepub.com/content/early/2016/01/07/0018726715609107?papetoc

32. Hurston, Z. (1990) Their Eyes Were Watching God: A Novel. New York: Perennial Library, Print

33. Khosrovani, M., P.H.D., & Ward, J. W., P.H.D. (2011). African Americans' perceptions of access to workplace opportunities: a survey of employees in Houston, Texas. Journal of Cultural Diversity, 18(4), 134-41.

34. Reid, A. (2010). The political implication of social capital. Harvard Journal of African American Public Policy, 16, 3-19.

35. Tonge, J. (2008). Barriers to networking for women in a UK professional service. Gender in Management, 23(7), 484-505.

36. Combs, G. M. (2003). The duality of race and gender for managerial African American women: Implications of informal social networks on career advancement. Human Resource Development Review, 2(4), 385-405.

37. Allman, E. (2017). Black women and the importance of safe spaces to our existence. Black Ballad. Retreived from https://Blackballad.co.uk/views-voices/Black-women-and-the-joy-of-creating-safe-spaces

38. Durlauf, S. N., & Fafchamps, M. (2004). Social capital. NBER Working Paper Series, 1-89. Retrieved from http://www.nber.org/papers/w10485

39. Vuong, A. (October 25, 2013). The role of people of color in the future workforce. Center for American Progress Blog. Retrieved from https://www.americanprogress.org/issues/immigration/news/2013/10/25/77924/the-role-of-people-of-color-in-the-future-workforce

40. Purdie-Vaughn's, V., & Eibach, R. P. (2008). Intersectional invisibility: The distinctive advantages and disadvantages of multiple subordinate-group identities. Sex Roles, 59(5-6), 377-391.

41. Brown, E., Haygood, M., McLean, J. (2010). The little Black book of success: Laws of leadership for Black women. One World Press

42. Gilbert, L. A., & Rossman, K. M. (1992). Gender and the mentoring process for women: Implications for professional development. Professional Psychology: Research and Practice, 23(3), 233-238.

43. Gonzáles-Figueroa, E., & Young, A. M. (2005). Ethnic identity and mentoring among Latinas in professional roles. Cultural Diversity and Ethnic Minority Psychology,11(3), 213-226.

44. Dow, R. S. (2014). Leadership responsibility in mentoring organization newcomers. Journal of Management Policy and Practice,15(1), 104-112.

45. Green, M.P. (2015). Creative mentorship and career-building strategies. Oxford University Press.

46. Hite, L. M. (2004). Black and white women managers: Access to opportunity. Human Resource Development Quarterly, 15(2), 131-146.

    b. Gonzáles-Figueroa, E., & Young, A. M. (2005). Ethnic identity and mentoring among Latinas in professional roles. Cultural Diversity and Ethnic Minority Psychology, 11(3), 213-226.

47. The Key Role of Sponsorship. Sandford SLAC https://inclusion.slac.stanford.edu/sites/inclusion.slac.stanford.edu/files/The_Key_Role_of_a_Sponsorship_for_Diverse_Talent.pdf

48. Beckwith, L. Carter, D. and Peters, T. (2016). The Underrepresentation of African American Women in Executive Leadership: What's Getting in the Way? The Journal of Business Quarterly 7(4)

49. Eagly, A. H., & Chin, J. L. (2010). Diversity and leadership in a changing world. The American Psychologist, 65(3), 216.

50. Catalyst. (2014). Feeling different: Being the "Other" in US workplaces. Retrieved from http://www.catalyst.org/system/files/feeling_different_being_the_other_in_us_workplaces.pdf

51. Creswell, J.W. (2015). A concise introduction to mixed methods research. Sage Publications.

52. Luthans, F., Youssef, C. M., & Avolio, B. J. (2007). Psychological capital: Developing the human competitive edge. New York, NY, US: Oxford University Press.

53. Bandura, A. (1997). Self-efficacy: The exercise of control. New York, NY, US: W H Freeman/Times Books/ Henry Holt & Co.

54. Morgan Roberts, L., Mayo, A., Ely, R., & Thomas, D. (2018). Beating the Odds: What Black women know about getting to the top. Harvard Business Review. Retrieved from https://hbr.org/2018/03/beating-the-odds

55. Beheshtifar, M. (2013). Organizational optimism: A considerable issue to success. Journal of Social Issues & Humanities, 1(6).

56. Creswell, J. (2013). Qualitative inquiry and research design: Choosing among the five approaches (third edition). Thousand Oaks, CA: Sage.

ABOUT THE AUTHOR

Dr. Waajida L. Small is the founder and CEO of Capital Conscious U LLC, a leadership development firm focused on helping career and entrepreneur women of color find and align their purpose with their careers and business. Over the past 15 years as a human resources leader and executive, Dr. Small has helped international organizations design and implement strategies to attract, develop, and retain top talent. She has also held multiple service roles including advisory board member for Rutgers University's Center for Innovation Big Data Certificate Program, Director, Strategic Partnerships for the Black Doctoral Network (BDN), and appointed co-chair of the Foundation Administrators Network with Philanthropy New York.

Dr. Small is passionate about helping women of color thrive in the workplace, in their businesses, and the world. Her work as a member, speaker and volunteer with organizations such as the United Nations Association Southern NY State Division Young Professionals, IMPACT Leadership 21 Emerging Global Leaders Circle Mentorship, Black Women of Influence, Wonder Women Tech, Women Future, The Black Girl Project, and the International Association of Women, has allowed her to broaden her span of scope to impact the lives of women across the globe.

Dr. Small is a firm believer that everyone can find, live, and work in their purpose. Her purpose is to help cultivate leaders who create spaces for women of color to thrive, be empowered to be their authentic selves, and lift as they climb. Using platforms such as her blog Living, Learning, Leading and her weekly podcast Leading with Purpose, Dr. Small provides insight into the real-life experiences of women of color in the workforce and coaches and teaches strategies and best practices to position women of color for success.

Dr. Small earned a doctorate in Human Capital Management with a research emphasis on women of color and leadership. She is also a Certified Purpose Leader (CPL), Certified Human Capital Strategist (HCS) and Certified Professional Coach (CPC) with specialties in career, executive, and spiritual coaching. She lives in New York with her husband, Christopher.

www.ingramcontent.com/pod-product-compliance
Lightning Source LLC
Chambersburg PA
CBHW020114240426
43673CB00001B/27